GARLAND STUDIES IN

AMERICAN POPULAR HISTORY AND CULTURE

edited by

JEROME NADELHAFT
UNIVERSITY OF MAINE

A GARLAND SERIES

AIDS, SOCIAL CHANGE, AND THEATER

PERFORMANCE AS PROTEST

CINDY J. KISTENBERG

GARLAND PUBLISHING, INC.
NEW YORK & LONDON / 1995

Library of Congress Cataloging-in-Publication Data

AIDS, social change, and theater : performance as protest / Cindy
J. Kistenberg
    p.   cm. — (Garland studies in American popular history
and culture)
    Includes bibliographical references and index.
    ISBN 0-8153-2159-7
    1. AIDS (Diseases) and the arts—United States.
I. Kistenberg, Cindy J., 1964–   . II. Series.
NX180.A36A37 1995
700—dc20   95-34639

Printed on acid-free, 250-year-life paper
Manufactured in the United States of America

Contents

Acknowledgments

I am indebted to a number of people for their assistance and support during the various phases of this project.

To the Communication Faculty at the University of North Carolina at Chapel Hill who helped develop my interest in rhetoric and performance studies, and pointed me in the right direction. Special thanks to Bill Balthrop, Robbie Cox, Paul Ferguson, Martha Nell Hardy, Beverly Long, and Della Pollock.

To the Speech Communication Faculty at Louisiana State University, and especially Renee Edwards, Mary Frances HopKins, Andrew King, and Kenneth Zagacki for providing feedback, insight, support, and encouragement during the initial phases of this work.

To all my colleagues and friends at the University of Houston-Downtown. Special thanks go to Brenetta Brooks, Jean DeWitt, Michael Dressman, Kirk Hagen, Kimberley Hause, Dan Jones, Tom Lyttle, Lloyd Matzner, Dean Minix, Pat Mosier, Hank Roubicek, Deborah Shelley, Margaret Shelton, Lisa Waldner-Haugrud, and Deloris Wanguri for added support, assistance, and encouragement.

To some very special people who, just by knowing them, have made my life more complete and this study markedly better: Ruth Laurion Bowman, Ann Chisholm, Randall Czarlinsky, Robert Drell, Cathy Ershler, Troy Faldyn, Kirk Fuoss, Jonathan Gray, Monty Hagler, Darlene Hantzis, Shari Harris, Randall Hill, Roger Kaplan, Danny Kent, Ken Kimsey, Karen Mitchell, Marjorie Ng, Sergio Pernas, Mike Pinkus, Katy Pollock, Charla Markham Shaw, Teresa Schaefer, Marvin and Arlene Shelsky, Jory Stein, and Haylee and Steven Travis.

To Rob McKenzie (my editor), Elspeth Hart (my production editor), Karin Badger (who designed the cover), and Jason Goldfarb (the Word Perfect genius) at Garland Publishing; and to Gary Jarvis, who provided the photograph for the cover. I could not have done it without all of your help.

To the members of my family—Ronna, Ira, and Robert Kistenberg—not only for their love, understanding, and patience but also for their continued interest and assistance with this project.

Finally I wish to thank the two people who, next to my family, have been the most significant influences on me throughout my years in higher education. Without them this project would not have existed. To Lawrence Rosenfeld at the University of North Carolina at Chapel Hill who taught me to write, research, and without whom I would not be where I am now. To Michael Bowman at Louisiana State University who taught me not only to believe in the power of language, but to believe in my ability to use it. I consider myself privileged to have these two brilliant teachers/scholars in my life as mentors and friends. They have helped me believe in myself and my abilities, and have shaped my professional career. I hope some day I will have as great an impact on someone's life as they have had on mine. I am indebted to you both forever.

This study is dedicated to all people living with HIV/AIDS, those who have died, and the people all over the world fighting to end this crisis. It is my hope that this book will soon become part of a chapter in a closed book on what *was* the AIDS crisis.

AIDS, Social Change, and Theater

I

Introduction

An utterance is legitimated or disregarded according to its place of
production and so, in large part, the history of political struggle has
been the history of the attempts made to control significant sites of
assembly and spaces of discourse.[1]

It is the morning of July 3, 1981. A group of men is gathered
on the porch of a beach house in New York City. One of the men is
reading to his friends an article in the *New York Times* entitled "Rare
Cancer Seen in 41 Homosexuals." One jokingly replies, "It's probably
from using poppers." Another says, "This is like the CIA trying to scare
us out of having sex."

Although the above scenario is taken from the movie *Longtime
Companion*, a fictional account of the effects of the AIDS crisis on the
lives of gay men in New York City, these responses are probably not
too different from what many gay men were saying when the *New York
Times* introduced to the public what was eventually to be named
Acquired Immune Deficiency Syndrome, or AIDS.[2] However, as the
movie continues, this "rare cancer" no longer seems a joke to these men;
rather, it becomes an issue that invades each of their lives.

Today, almost fifteen years after the *Times* article, it is
difficult, especially in the United States, to imagine finding someone
who knows nothing about AIDS. Rarely does a day go by without an
AIDS-related story appearing in the newspapers or on television. With
reports indicating that ten million people worldwide are infected with
Human Immunodeficiency Virus (HIV)—the virus that causes
AIDS—and no immediate cure in sight, the AIDS issue has the potential
to affect every person in the world.[3]

The growing number of persons affected by AIDS has led a number of groups and individuals to propose and enact various solutions for dealing with the crisis. The medical community, schools, churches, the government, and AIDS activists have all addressed the AIDS issue in a variety of ways. For example, a number of religious organizations, the Catholic Church being the most prominent, preach sexual abstinence. Some schools dispense condoms to their students, while other organizations distribute sterile hypodermic needles to drug users. The government has been involved with a variety of issues ranging from mandatory AIDS testing, education, to increased funding for research. But, while the public's attention to AIDS has increased, it is relatively easy to find people who are misinformed about some aspect of AIDS. And in spite of efforts to address the AIDS problem, the epidemic is still growing at alarming rates.

According to many cultural critics, these misconceptions result from how AIDS has been linguistically constructed by the mass media and various medical and scientific institutions. Paula Treichler, for example, attributes the cultural or social construction of AIDS to certain cultural narratives that have been created and perpetuated by biomedical discourse. Such narratives constitute the reality of AIDS. She suggests that as new narratives and meanings are created, we must ask a number of questions:

> How and why is knowledge about AIDS being produced in the way that it is?
> Who is contributing to the process of knowledge production? To whom and by whom is this knowledge disseminated?
> What are the practical and material consequences of any new interpretation? Who benefits? Who loses?
> On what grounds are facts and truth being claimed?[4]

Essentially, what Treichler is suggesting is that we need to look at the language that is used to create what AIDS means and determine whose interests are served by these conceptualizations. By reframing the AIDS crisis in this way, researchers such as Treichler argue that AIDS is not simply an objective biological entity, but a site of political struggle between various institutions, groups, and individuals—a struggle that plays itself out in language. Treichler states, "we must examine how language itself produces what we think we know; if we are to intervene, language is one place where that intervention must take place."[5] Simon Watney takes Treichler's comment a step further by arguing, "Language plays a central role in determining public perceptions of all aspects of AIDS, and its many consequences around the world. Language shapes attitudes, and beliefs, which in turn inform behavior."[6] Thus, Treichler, Watney, and others suggest that by changing the language that is used to construct AIDS, it is possible to alter actions towards persons with AIDS, as well as the circumstances in which those with HIV/AIDS live.

The purpose of this study is to explore the political rhetoric of selected performances that have emerged out of the AIDS crisis and to examine how these performances attempt to intervene in this political struggle. The very nature of these performances, embedded as they are within the discourse surrounding the crisis, requires that they be viewed as additional attempts to intervene in the crisis. By focusing on conventional and alternative forms of performance attempting to intervene in the crisis, this study seeks to provide additional insight into how meanings and values can be maintained, challenged, or changed through the performance act.

Performances dealing with AIDS present us with various representations of AIDS. Each of these representations helps define—or redefine—what AIDS is. As Brian Wallis explains:

> [R]epresentations are those artificial (though seemingly immutable) constructions through which we apprehend the world: conceptual representations such as images, languages, definitions: which include and construct more social representations such as race and gender. Although such constructions often depend on a material form in the real world, representations constantly are posed as natural "facts" and their misleading plenitude obscures our apprehension of reality. Our access to reality is mediated by a gauze of representation.[7]

In his book *The Politics of Representation*, Michael Shapiro explains how even photographs, which are commonly taken to be "pure," unmediated copies of reality, are, in actuality, artificial constructs with particular meanings and values that constitute, as well as reflect, reality.

When we begin to view these photographic representations *as* representations, we can begin to understand how photography can be utilized to challenge or maintain dominant values. He argues:

> To discern the political rhetoric of photography it is necessary, rather, to look at photographic statements on the basis of their tendency to either reproduce dominant forms of discourse, which help circulate existing systems of power, authority, and exchange or to look at them on the basis of their tendency to provoke critical analysis, to denaturalize what is unproblematically accepted and to offer thereby an avenue for politicizing problematics. Taken in this latter sense, photography always plays a politically radical role when it opens up forms of questions about power and authority which are closed or silenced within the most frequently circulated and authoritative discursive practices.[8]

Shapiro's ideas about photography are also true of AIDS performances: representations of AIDS in performances are always in dialogue with other representations. These performances thus become a dialogue between or among competing representations. All representations—whether produced by the media, medicine, the government, or performances—determine the way we think about AIDS. Thus, following Shapiro's advice, in this study I look at performances emerging out of the AIDS crisis in terms of their tendency to reproduce existing systems of power and authority by perpetuating dominant representations of AIDS, or as provoking critical analysis, i.e., challenging these dominant representations by "re-signifying AIDS."

This chapter is divided into four sections. The first section examines the political rhetoric of the AIDS crisis in order to understand the dominant representations of AIDS to which the performances described in this study respond. This section explains the social construction of AIDS as a site of political struggle—as a struggle between "official" (or dominant) and "unofficial" discourses. The second section explains the difficulty of challenging this dominant discourse and concludes by raising the question guiding this study: Why are various groups turning to performance as a means to challenge the dominant culture's construction of AIDS? The third section addresses this question further by looking at performance as a political tool. The final section previews the remaining chapters, presents the limitations of the study, and explains its significance.

POLITICALLY CONSTRUCTING THE AIDS CRISIS

The difficulty of providing any critical/historical account of AIDS is compounded by recent findings that AIDS has been with us much longer than most people think.[9] We may never know how, when, or where AIDS originated. Thus, rather than presenting *the* history of the AIDS crisis, I present *a* critical history of the crisis based on my readings of a number of texts. I do not claim to present every significant event, nor do I claim to be objective in the events I have selected. My aim in this section is to explain why many view AIDS as a political, as well as a health, issue, and to provide a context for reading those performances that attempt to deal with the politics of AIDS.

Dennis Altman points to what is arguably the most significant element in the political rhetoric of AIDS:

> Even though AIDS is in no intrinsic sense "a gay disease," the fact that, at least in the Western World, it has been primarily experienced by male homosexuals has shaped the entire discourse surrounding the disease. . . . [T]he more a disease is experienced collectively, particularly by an already stigmatized group, the clearer will be its political dimensions.[10]

This relationship between homosexuals and what would be called AIDS is first found in the *New York Times* article previously mentioned. And, in January of 1982, the term "GRID" (gay-related immune deficiency) became a popular, albeit unofficial, name for the syndrome. It was not until the fall of 1982 that "AIDS" became the official term used to describe what was then largely viewed as a sexually transmitted disease which afflicted homosexuals due to their sexual practices and life-style.[11] Even though the acronym AIDS, unlike GRID, does not equate the illness with homosexuals, the original publicity created a link between homosexuals and AIDS that still remains today. As Altman explains, "The fact that the first reported cases were exclusively among gay men was to affect the whole future conceptualization of AIDS."[12] Essentially, AIDS was, and still is, constructed as "a gay disease."[13]

It was also in 1982 that AIDS was discovered in non-homosexuals. However, these non-homosexuals were found to share certain traits that made it convenient to lump them into groups, or "at risk" groups. These groups included intravenous drug users, Haitians, and hemophiliacs. As a result, those "at risk" for AIDS became known as the "four H's"—homosexuals, heroin addicts, Haitians, and hemophiliacs.[14] And while it is plausible that this discovery could have challenged the exclusive relationship between homosexual practices and AIDS, it led ironically to a number of additional problems for the homosexual community.

Before AIDS was found in other groups, homosexuals, who were already marginalized, were viewed by some as deserving whatever they got. The Reverend Jerry Falwell, for example, claimed that "AIDS is God's judgment against a society that does not live by His rules."[15] Later, when it became apparent that AIDS had spread into the "general population," we begin to find the term "innocent victim" as a means through which, for example, babies and those who contracted AIDS through blood transfusions could be differentiated from those who were infected through chosen behaviors (e.g., anal sex and IV drug use). Thus, blaming *some* of the "victims" became the primary way the dominant culture began to deal with AIDS. Altman explains, "The equation of AIDS with gay men carried with it a strain of blaming gays for the introduction and spread of the disease, and the concomitant idea that others who fell sick were somehow 'innocent victims.'"[16]

Randy Shilts suggests that the history of the AIDS crisis is separated into two distinct time periods. These periods, he argues, are separated by the announcement, made in the summer of 1985, that Rock Hudson had AIDS:

> Rock Hudson riveted America's attention upon this deadly new threat for the first time, and his diagnosis became a demarcation that would separate the history of America before AIDS from the history that came after.[17]

Here Shilts is referring to the amount of attention AIDS received in the mass media after the announcement that Hudson had AIDS. However, this increase in attention did not change the equation between AIDS and homosexuality. Indeed, it could be argued that the equation was only reinforced because we learned that Rock Hudson was gay. Although, initially, attempts were made by various organizations, particularly gay and AIDS organizations, to argue that he was not gay (his infection was blamed on a blood transfusion he had had years earlier), by July 25, 1985, Rock Hudson's sexual orientation was on the front page of most major newspapers. As Shilts explains, the man who had "personified wholesome American masculinity" was now a gay man with AIDS.[18] While Hudson's death from AIDS did draw more attention to the issue, when it became public knowledge that he was gay, a number of people who initially had thought "If he isn't safe, no one is safe" were quite relieved.

While AIDS has received significantly more publicity since Rock Hudson's death, and while many now realize that it is no longer confined to certain groups of people, the way AIDS was initially presented and discussed by the medical community, the government, and the media forced AIDS to become a political issue. Cindy Patton explains:

> There is a common belief that AIDS information giving is politically neutral, but both the progressive AIDS activists and the right wing mean different things when they assert the same facts. Fact-based language is used both by the right, which views mainstream AIDS education as a gay plot, and by liberals who want to depoliticize AIDS. But we can't simply depoliticize AIDS by using neutral sounding terms. In fact, in the current landscape, we cannot depoliticize AIDS at all.[19]

One way to understand the politics of AIDS is to look at it as a struggle between official and unofficial representations that attempt to determine what AIDS is. Simon Watney provides the best understanding of the problems inherent in the dominant construction of AIDS:

> . . . official AIDS information participates actively in the ideological foreground of all Western societies, seemingly

validating social values and boundaries with the full authority of
"science," and excluding whole population groups from what Stuart
Hall has described as "the imaginary community of the nation."[20]

The "official AIDS information" to which Watney refers seems to fall
into four categories; that is, the official or dominant discourse has
constructed AIDS as: (1) a homosexual affliction; (2) a sexually
transmitted disease; (3) an affliction of drug users; and (4) a
scientific/medical problem.

First, perhaps the most significant element of the dominant
construction of AIDS is the link between gay men and AIDS. Especially
in the United States, AIDS was most often found in groups of people,
most notably, male homosexuals. Ironically, the visibility and sexual
freedom gays experienced after the Stonewall riot contributed to their
being blamed for the spread of AIDS.

The Stonewall riot occurred in New York City on June 27,
1969, after police officers raided a gay bar called the Stonewall Inn on
Christopher Street.[21] Instead of the usual, passive response to such raids,
the bar patrons gathered outside the bar, and soon a large crowd had
formed. The people in the crowd began shouting at the police and
violence erupted. The police called in reinforcements to control the
crowd; however, the riot continued through the next day. "Gay Power"
was written on walls along Christopher Street, and the police violently
attacked a number of the protesters in an attempt to control them. In
response, a number of the protesters attacked police cars in the area,
threw rocks and bottles, started fires in garbage cans, and "cries of 'Gay
Power!' rang in the streets, as the police, numbering more than 400, did
battles with a crowd estimated at more than 2000."[22]

According to D'Emilio, the Stonewall riot had a significant
impact on the lives of gays and lesbians.[23] One result of the riot was the
formation of the Gay Liberation Front and, later, the creation of gay
liberation groups on various campuses throughout the country. And
these groups, much like various women's rights organizations, have
been attempting to legitimate homosexuality and lesbianism as visible
alternative, but equally valid, life styles. Another result of the Stonewall
Riot was more sexual freedom, including the increased availability of
sexual encounters. Altman suggests that while we cannot know precisely

what led to changes in homosexual behavior during the 1970s, increased use of recreational drugs, as well as the growth of bath houses and sex clubs, were probably partially responsible for these changes.[24] Thus, the emergence of gay rights and the increase of sexual freedom that emerged in the late 1960s are often cited as reasons to explain both the visibility and the spread of AIDS among homosexuals.

Because researchers knew more about the life styles of homosexuals, it was easy for them to attribute AIDS to sexual practices, particularly the promiscuity, of gay men. In the early 1980s, when it was realized that those falling ill were "known homosexuals," researchers began looking into the specific practices of gay men to determine why. The cause receiving most of the attention was promiscuity. As a result, promiscuity became viewed as the *cause* of AIDS, in both medicine and the media, suggesting not only that if a person was not promiscuous she or he could not get AIDS, but that everyone who was affected had been promiscuous.[25]

Another irony, although one that cannot be so clearly linked to gay liberation, is that gay men as a whole are more financially stable than the other groups that have been affected by AIDS. Altman explains,

> [I]t was the comparative advantage enjoyed by gay men in access to medical care that meant the first cases were diagnosed among them, and probably means that there remains severe underreporting of AIDS, perhaps among other groups in the United States and Europe, but almost certainly in the Third World.[26]

In other words, the financial stability of gay men, in comparison to others with AIDS-related symptoms, made them far more visible to the medical community. Their access to the medical community helped create the link between homosexuals and AIDS.

One final irony worth mentioning is that by the early 1980s homosexuals were already organized—another effect of the Stonewall riot. There were a number of groups already established, and these were among the first to begin lobbying for research and support. Altman argues that "the very assertiveness of gay groups, which are comparatively well off in skills and resources, merely strengthens the image of AIDS as a gay disease, and the need to mobilize their community means that gay leaders reinforce that connection."[27]

Attributing AIDS to gay men also serves another function: it helps perpetuate certain cultural narratives that are already firmly entrenched in our society. In her article "Every Virus Tells a Story," Judith Williamson states, "AIDS has not 'provoked' all the hysterical responses to it—it has entered an *already* homophobic, blame-oriented culture obsessed with particular types of closed narratives."[28] Homosexuality, she explains, interferes with one of these narratives, the family narrative, which tell us we should "grow up, get married, have children, repeat . . .," because the homosexual narrative does not follow this particular sequence of events. The homosexual's "interference" in this narrative makes her or him the perfect scapegoat for AIDS and helps maintain the dominance of the family narrative. She concludes, "So one way or another the AIDS discourse of our society is structured and coded precisely to fend off transgression . . ."[29] And fending off transgression is also apparent in the second and third elements of the dominant construction of AIDS—the link between AIDS and sex, and AIDS and IV drug use—since each of these behaviors is not part of the narrative in which the ideal life is supposed to unfold.

The dominant discourse has reinforced the link between AIDS and sex by continuously referring to AIDS as a sexually transmitted disease. This linkage has provided many moralists with ammunition to use against persons with AIDS. As Sander Gilman explains, "The idea of the person afflicted with [a Sexually Transmitted Disease], one of the most potent in the repertory of images of the stigmatized patient, became the paradigm through which people with AIDS were understood and categorized."[30] Although it was soon learned that AIDS was linked to a retrovirus named HIV, *and* that it could be transmitted by means other than sexual contact, rather than viewing AIDS as a "viral disease," it was characterized (and therefore perceived) as a sexually transmitted disease (STD), linking it to others STDs (e.g., syphilis).[31]

Mary Poovey provides a concise explanation of the problems that emerge when AIDS is viewed mainly as a sexually transmitted disease:

> As long as AIDS is conceptualized primarily by one mode of transmission, for example—as a *sexual* disease—it will belong to the signifying chains that include, on the one hand, syphilis, gonorrhea, and hepatitis, and on the other, transgression, sin, dirtiness, contagion, death. Sexual intercourse is only one means by which AIDS is transmitted . . . but because this mode of transmission has dominated discussions of the disease, AIDS now seems to be bound up to the moralistic equation of the 1980s: sex = sin = death.[32]

Thus, the dominant discourse on AIDS has created a linkage between homosexuals and AIDS, and AIDS and sexually transmitted disease, that has served to increase both the stigmatization and marginalization of homosexuals and PWAs since the AIDS crisis began. These representations are one reason why homosexuals became the scapegoats for AIDS, and they may also help to explain why various institutions (e.g., medicine and the government) have been slow to respond to the crisis.[33]

It is important to note, however, that these representations allow other groups significantly affected by AIDS to be ignored. For some critics, the emphasis on homosexuality in the dominant construction of AIDS (where homosexuality is defined solely in terms of sexual practices) has exposed the racism, sexism, and classism that exist in our society. As I mentioned earlier, not only were gay men already organized as a group, they also had greater access to health care, making them more visible in the eyes of the public. But, as a result, others affected by AIDS—persons of color, IV drug users, and women (often those of lower socioeconomic status)—have remained largely invisible, as they always have been, to the dominant culture. Watney explains:

> If Aids [sic] is to be a metaphor for anything, it is up to us to make sure that in time it becomes regarded as a glaring example of how the ill may be victimised [sic] far beyond their physical symptoms, and of how far a deeply racist and sexist society will go to prosecute its own ends.[34]

Thus, the third element in the official construction of AIDS—the link between AIDS and IV drug use—has been downplayed. It is included as one aspect of the dominant construction of AIDS because IV drug use and unsafe sexual practices are the emphasized modes of transmission for HIV, but such inclusion does not imply that drug users have received equal billing in the media's AIDS circus.

Like homosexuals, heroin users are viewed as deviants by the dominant culture; however, because drug users have less access to medical care and political institutions, and because they are often persons of lower socioeconomic status, they have been relatively ignored. As Patton explains, "Injecting drug users lacked the formal structures of the gay community . . . and there was rarely a social identity for drug users to understand themselves as a political constituency."[35] Thus, IV drug use is generally discussed in the dominant discourse as a means through which the virus can be transmitted, but those affected by AIDS through IV drug use are often ignored, except, of course, when their practices affect "the innocent" (babies).

Finally, the official discourse constructs AIDS as a scientific/medical problem—a disease. The problem with such a construction is two-fold. First, it ignores the fact that the term AIDS has both denotative and connotative meanings; it attempts to ignore or discount the connotations that are connected with the term AIDS—that AIDS is viewed as a "gay disease," an affliction of IV drug users, and a sexually transmitted disease—in favor of "fact-based" language, i.e., language that is "neutral," "objective," or "true." The second problem is related to the first: viewing AIDS as a scientific/medical problem tends to privilege the discourse of certain people over others. The experts (doctors, scientific researchers) are viewed as possessing the "truth" about AIDS, while lay people (AIDS activists, persons with AIDS, "victims," or "patients") are either subjected to these "truths" or expected to accept what the experts say as "truth." Or, in other words, the official discourse that constructs AIDS as a disease sets up a dichotomy between those who dispense and those who seek treatment—between those who know the truth and those who must learn it. However, the distinctions between the "experts" and "patients" or "victims" during the AIDS crisis has not always been as polarized as it is today.

Prior to Rock Hudson's disclosure, organizations working with AIDS were primarily funded by gay organizations. As Cindy Patton explains the financial stability of gay men and the relationship between gay men and the arts enhanced the development of private, non-profit AIDS organizations.[36] When AIDS entered the "heterosexual population" and the government realized that action must be taken, these organizations were approached by the government and treated as experts for dealing with AIDS. However, the increased attention to AIDS during 1985 also decreased the expertise of gay men. As Patton states, "[A]s government and media interest increased, gay men came to viewed largely as a special 'lobby' rather than as 'experts.'"[37]

While this example may appear irrelevant to scientific and medical discourse, it illustrates how the distinctions between "victims" and "experts" developed as a result of economic and political consideration, rather than from scientific or medical progress. Patton explains that when the government began funding AIDS organizations in 1985, several changes occurred within the structure of these organizations. These changes included the implementation of different hiring practices as well as the separation of agencies dealing with persons with AIDS and education. Education agencies were later divided into those focusing on "community education" and those concerned with "professional or general public education."[38] Patton notes:

> The new industry developed a vision of itself and of AIDS work that stood in sharp contrast to the early community activism, in which there were few distinctions between organizers, activists, people living with AIDS, and sympathetic medical workers. It inscribed a rigid role structure which constructed "victims," "experts," and "volunteers" as the *dramatis personae* in its story of AIDS.[39]

Thus, while AIDS was always viewed as a medical problem, government intervention led to significant changes in AIDS organizations and affected how all those involved with the AIDS crisis were viewed.

But what are the problems with calling people "AIDS victims?" Why is the term "victim" problematic? Jan Zita Grover suggests three problems inherent in the term's usage: (1) the fatalism, (2) the effect of cancellation, and (3) the negative psychological sense.[40] First, fatalism means that when people are referred to as victims, they become objects of pity and fear. Like the audience for a Greek tragedy, we may sympathize with the victim's plight, but there is nothing we can do to alter his or her fate. As Grover explains:

> Fatalism implies that nothing, or next to nothing, can be done about the cultural, social, and medical crises presented by AIDS. It denies the very possibility of all that is *in fact* being done by people living with AIDS and those working with them.[41]

Second, the effect of cancellation is a result of the fatalism associated with the term "victim." Essentially, the term "AIDS victim" transforms a living human being into a corpse. In contrast, the label "persons with AIDS" (PWA) or "persons living with AIDS" (PLWA) implies activity rather than passivity. Finally, psychological implications are perhaps the most obvious problem implied by the usage of the term "victim." Although the term, as it is defined by the dictionary, suggests that what has happened to the person labelled as such is accidental, a result of fate, there is a degree to which a person who believes she or he is a victim often blames her or himself.

Grover's discussion of the term victim makes it easy to explain why the dominant culture has adopted this term as a label for persons with AIDS. As I have already argued, AIDS is heavily linked to drug use and sexual practices. Thus, not only do "victims" get blamed for contracting AIDS through practices viewed as immoral or deviant, the term also often leads these people to blame themselves. Whether the blame is self- or other-oriented, the result is still the same—if people believe they are "victims," they are unlikely to engage in actions that will remedy their situation because they believe it was their actions that caused their affliction in the first place. And, of course, the notion of blaming the victim also leads to the creation of a dichotomy between "innocent" and "non-innocent victims" of AIDS previously mentioned. For the "innocent victims," blame can be directed toward those who are believed to have infected them, and it can, as in the case of all "victims," keep them passively awaiting their fate.

Persons with AIDS reject the label "AIDS victim" for reasons similar to those expressed above. At the lesbian and gay health conference in 1983, PWAs issued what was called the "Denver Principles," which included the following statement: "We condemn attempts to label us as "victims," which implies defeat, and we are only occasionally "patients," which implies passivity, helplessness, and dependence upon the care of others.[42]

In summary, "AIDS victim" is a significant element in the dominant discourse surrounding AIDS because it allows issues of morality and deviancy to enter into the AIDS domain. As I stated earlier, it becomes one of the primary ways the dominant culture deals with the AIDS issue. And although objections have been raised by researchers, theorists, and PWAs, the dominant culture still persists in labelling people infected with AIDS as "victims."

In contrast to the "victims," in the medical/scientific construction of AIDS, we also have the "experts." These people include those dispensing treatment (doctors) and those studying the virus (medical researchers). These are the people, Patton argues, who are privileged with the right to say what AIDS is. Science, she maintains, has been so valorized, especially since the last century, that we seldom question its methods and results:

> The dominance of science as *the* logical paradigm rationalizes systems of social control which predate the HIV epidemic, especially systems which silence or distort the speech and culture of "minority communities" by constructing them as lacking in the forms of discourse which enable people to "make sense."[43]

The number of challenges that have been made to the idea of science as "objective" by both PWAs and AIDS activists have not changed society's view that science provides us with the most important information about AIDS. The mistakes and controversies that have occurred within the scientific community over the past decade have done nothing to alter the credibility we have afforded science during the AIDS crisis. As Patton explains:

> Despite highly publicized stories alleging that research scientist Bob Gallo stole the virus from his counterpart Luc Montagne; despite

> revelations that Burroughs-Wellcome lost track of over a thousand (nearly 1/4th) of its compassionate-release AZT trial subjects; despite the inability of international research after nearly a decade to produce an anti-viral agent or immune booster that effectively and predictably halts HIV; despite the apparent failure of tens of thousands of scientists to make significant headway against HIV infection; despite all of these highly publicized assaults on the progress of research, science as an ideal has increased its stature and successfully claimed itself to be above politics.[44]

But these "experts" determine and tell us the facts, while the "victims" are silenced. Because the "victims" are living with AIDS, they are considered too biased, too close to the issues, to have a voice in AIDS care or treatment.

Of course, all of the previous information is not included to invalidate many of the important discoveries made through scientific research. Nor is it intended to argue that the "experts" are inherently evil. This discussion is provided to explain how science as a system is founded on notions of objectivity, which, in turn, leads us to believe that what scientists have to say is inherently more valuable than those with AIDS/HIV. Treichler further validates this claim:

> Although physicians and scientists have unique and valuable contributions to make, they are not inherently better informed than AIDS activists, nor is their knowledge more complicated than that which informed patients can bring to the treatment scene.[45]

The problems with biomedical discourse and its dissemination into society have led PWAs and AIDS activists to become AIDS experts themselves and to challenge many of the practices of the medical community. Treichler explains that these people have come to understand the politics of the government, technology and science, biomedical research, economics, and the importance of self-education.[46] In addition, rather than dismissing technology, they have seized "it for progressive political purposes and for the deployment of science and scientific theory in everyday life."[47]

THE PROBLEMS OF INTERVENING

Although AIDS activists have had some success intervening in the AIDS crisis, especially in regards to treatment, the amount of time it took for such intervention to be successful suggests how hard it is to challenge the dominant constructions of AIDS. These representations allow heterosexuals to feel safe—to read information on AIDS and say, in effect, "I'm not promiscuous, homosexual, or a drug user, and therefore AIDS is not a threat to me." As I have suggested, these dominant representations of AIDS are widely accepted and established, posing a number of problems for those who are attempting to challenge them.

The first problem is that what counts as the "facts" or "truths" about AIDS are accepted and presented by the scientific/medical community. The information provided by this community is culturally constructed as objective, scientific, and therefore more valuable than the information disseminated by individuals, especially when these individuals, who are often members of marginalized groups, are perceived as pursuing their own interests. The opinions, beliefs, and feelings of those with AIDS are constituted as less important, less relevant than the information presented by the scientific/medical community. In other words, the scientific/medical community has been afforded the power to speak; their messages are accepted as truth; they are the experts. Because scientific research is based on the verification and re-verification of various findings, the scientist is viewed as an authority—as speaking for science as a discipline that already has the power to speak because it is viewed as being objective. The person with AIDS is seen as speaking for him/herself or a particular community, as being subjective.

But we cannot deny that there are some persons with AIDS whose voices do get heard. In an article on AIDS and the media, John Gallagher poses the question, "[T]o what extent do the media need a heterosexual angle even to report on AIDS?"[48] The "faces of AIDS," the ones with which we can associate a name, are always heterosexual and almost always the "innocent." Watney makes a similar point when he states, "'Human interest' criteria may make space for pathos-laden stories concerning 'AIDS victims,' as long as they happen to be heterosexual."[49]

The two most notable examples are Ryan White and Kimberly Bergalis. Ryan White was the first widely publicized "innocent victim." A teen-age hemophiliac who was diagnosed with AIDS in 1984 and died in 1990, Ryan White attracted a great deal of attention to the AIDS issue. The second widely publicized "innocent victim" was Kimberly Bergalis, the Florida woman who allegedly contracted HIV from her dentist. Gallagher explains that after White's death "the press had not settled upon a national AIDS figure. Bergalis filled that void" because she was white, middle-class, and heterosexual.[50] Her voice was heard. Although the chance of contracting the virus from a health care worker is estimated to be "as low as one in 2,631,579," Bergalis's case led to congressional debates regarding testing of health-care workers.[51]

In an article entitled "AIDS 'Heroes' and 'Villains,'" Tom Ehrenfeld discusses the politics of the Kimberly Bergalis case:

> I find Kimberly Bergalis's personal story tragic beyond words. But I find the way she is being used politically just as horrifying. There's a larger picture obscured by the sorrow Bergalis evokes in her campaign. Why is it when a young heterosexual like her gets sick from AIDS, the floor of the Senate rings with action, while when homosexuals and drug users suffer they are insulted, quarantined and hated?[52]

Other persons with AIDS do not get the opportunity to have their voices heard. And, when their voices are heard, the mode of transmission takes precedence over what they have to say about treatment and care for persons with AIDS. Causes, rather than cures and care, are emphasized.

Finally, of course, we have Magic Johnson. On November 7, 1991, Earvin "Magic" Johnson disclosed that he had tested HIV—positive. His disclosure could be viewed as the third major development in the AIDS crisis. While Johnson does not fall into the "innocent" category due to his admitted promiscuity, his status as a sports hero and heterosexual allowed his voice to be heard. He is, as the subtitle of one article reads, "a true American hero" who has joined "the battle against the deadly AIDS virus."[53]

However, as tennis star Martina Navratilova argues, if she had disclosed that she had tested positive for HIV, the response would have been much different. Although a number of other athletes have died, they were "pushed aside because they got it from drugs or they were gay."[54] And although sexual promiscuity is not condoned by the dominant culture, Johnson's status as a sports figure allowed him to become a spokesperson for AIDS.

When Johnson initially announced his status, he vehemently argued for people to practice safe sex. During an appearance on the *Arsenio Hall Show* he asserted, "I want everyone to understand that having the HIV virus that I want everybody to practice safe sex, and that's using condoms and . . . be aware of what's going on." A few weeks later, in an interview with Connie Chung, it was clear that he had apparently changed his mind when more than once he claimed, "The safest sex is no sex." The reason for this shift is unclear. Perhaps he changed his rhetoric to be more in line with that of the current administration, or perhaps he changed it for some other reason. But regardless of his reasons, Magic Johnson, arguably the most visible person with HIV, modified his position to conform with the dominant discourse surrounding the AIDS crisis.

Because he was infected through heterosexual contact, his disclosure had the potential to do what Rock Hudson's disclosure failed to accomplish—to make heterosexuals realize that AIDS is not a "gay disease." However, the mass media attempted to "contain" AIDS by focusing on Johnson's promiscuity. For example, on November 25, 1991, the cover of *Time* included the phrase "The Promiscuous World of Pro Sports" and contained an article on sports "groupies." *Sports Illustrated* included an article discussing the promiscuity of professional athletes.[55] The *National Enquirer*, *Globe*, and *Star* also contained stories about Johnson's promiscuity. And, of course, rumors regarding Johnson's sexual orientation were discussed by the mass media. Thus, with the mass media qualifying Johnson's HIV status by presenting these rumors and focusing on issues of promiscuity, the impact of his disclosure was potentially decreased.

Because the mass media assumes a heterosexual audience, heterosexual stories are the ones that are most common (e.g., the man who contracts HIV through a blood transfusion and subsequently infects his wife and their unborn child), and heterosexual voices are allowed to be heard. Although the number of heterosexuals in the United States with HIV/AIDS is small,[56] especially in comparison to the number of gay men, heterosexuals are allowed to speak and, as the Bergalis case illustrates, have an impact on public policy. When others speak, members of ACT UP, for example, the mass media makes sure that what they have to say does not contradict or challenge dominant beliefs and values. The influence of television is enormous. And when it comes to teaching, television is a tool that is quite effective. Baker sums up its power quite well when he states that "no other medium takes words and moving images directly into people's living rooms, kitchens, and bedrooms; no other medium has so much potential to influence attitudes, for better or worse."

The difficulty of intervening in the AIDS crisis is primarily a result of society's reliance on the experts to dictate what AIDS is. These are the people who speak the "truth," and these "truths" serve as the means through which public policy decisions are made concerning funding, education, treatment. Their "truths" come to us through various forms of mass media. But, as I have suggested, their truths also expose the racism, classism, sexism, and homophobia in our society.

Persons attempting to intervene in the AIDS crisis have used a variety of performance-centered strategies. For example, both *As Is* and *The Normal Heart* are plays that have been presented in conventional theaters and have served a cathartic function for gay men during the AIDS epidemic.[57] Other strategies utilized to deal with the crisis have involved non-traditional performances such as marches, demonstrations, and performance art. The AIDS Coalition to Unleash Power (ACT-UP) has been extremely visible over the last few years in its attempts to affect public policy and to present a more accurate picture of the AIDS crisis. In addition, the NAMES Project (the AIDS Memorial Quilt) has played a key role not only as a cathartic experience, but it has also made people aware that gay men are not the only people affected by AIDS. Finally, the works of performance artists Tim Miller and Karen Finley also have received some attention; however, this attention was primarily because they were denied funding by the National Endowment for the Arts due to the controversial nature of their work.

Each of these projects represents an attempt to discursively intervene in the AIDS crisis. However, given society's reliance on the "experts" and more "instrumental" forms of discourse, it would seem that performances would be ineffective tools for challenging the dominant representations of AIDS. So the questions that must be answered are: Why have people selected performance-centered strategies? Do performances offer possibilities for intervening in the crisis? Can performances do what speeches and other traditional forms of rhetoric cannot?

Furthermore, in order to determine the effectiveness of these performances, we must understand what "effectiveness" means in relation to the AIDS crisis: Does it mean providing people with outlets for catharsis? Does it involve changing attitudes towards homosexuals and/or AIDS? Does it mean, as some activists argue, "putting drugs into bodies"? Or does it involve, as Treichler and others argue, intervening in the discursive practices that create distinctions between what is "true" and what is "false"?

As evidenced by the preceding discussion, recent critical/cultural studies of AIDS have been extremely critical of the "dominant" construction of AIDS. They have also been instrumental in challenging the way this discourse might be contested or resisted. As Patton argues:

> neither dialectical analysis nor "speaking out" (the articulation of previously foreclosed "personal" or "private" experiences characteristic of the new left, Black Power, feminist, and gay liberation movements) exhaust strategies of resistance; in the present situation, they may in fact impede them.[58]

In Patton's view, "speaking out" as a form of resistance only makes sense in terms of a unitary conception of power.[59] Given this conception of power, individuals or groups obtain power simply by articulating ideas or experiences that are normally silenced or ignored in society's "significant sites of assembly" or discursive forms.[60] Patton and other critics work from a different conception of power—power as network—which entails a different conception of resistance. Patton explains that this understanding of power appears "most often through 'cultural politics' or artistic interventions" and "attempts to deconstruct current discursive practices by signaling their complicity in covering up the more subtle aspects of the play of power, and by suggesting points of resistance." She concludes:

> In practice, this involves not speaking from any particular place, or speaking from shifting subject positions in order to make apparent who is subjected to repressive practices and where the reader sits in relation to those systems of power. Though these critiques cannot cancel out the effects of power in unitary forms, they can de-essentialize power metaphorized as epistemological center, thereby opening up space for marginalized voices and subversive, local practices of resistance.[61]

In Patton's terms, artistic interventions or "cultural politics" enable groups or individuals to challenge their status mainly by evading power to "de-essentialize" differences in power or authority based on identity. As we have seen, the rhetoric surrounding the AIDS crisis has essentialized the differences among persons with AIDS; identities and power relations have been established based on modes of transmission. Patton's discussion of power shows us the problems with identity politics and suggests how such configurations might be resisted.

Paula Treichler supports Patton's position and goes on to suggest a specific site where such resistance might be performed. In "AIDS, Homophobia, and Biomedical Discourse: An Epidemic of Signification," she argues that because AIDS is a linguistic construct—an effect of the discourse of medicine and science—resistance means working to challenge the representations of AIDS that have been created by these discourses:

> The name *AIDS* in part *constructs* the disease and helps make it intelligible. We cannot therefore look "through" language to determine what AIDS "really" is. Rather we must explore the site where such determinations *really* occur and intervene at the point where meaning is created: in language.[62]

Treichler further explains that while we often want to rely on science and medicine (as opposed to ourselves) as presenting the "reality" of AIDS to us, we must realize that "the AIDS epidemic—with its genuine potential for global devastation—is simultaneously an epidemic of a transmissible lethal disease and an epidemic of meanings or significations."[63]

Thus, it is Treichler's view that we cannot let scientific and medical discourse determine what AIDS really is, i.e., we cannot let their discourse determine the "facts" about AIDS. These discourses have created many assumptions that have been perpetuated for more than ten years and have prevented substantial resources from being devoted to both research and support for those with AIDS.

Most importantly, however, Treichler has also provided a means to understand social change as it is related to language. It is within language that "meanings" or "signifying systems" are created, and where the potential for social change exists. Language is viewed as the key to understanding the means through which the dominant culture asserts its control over the individual—as the place where certain meanings are privileged and others are either opposed or ignored. As Graeme Turner explains:

> language looms as the most essential of concepts, either in its own right or through being appropriated as a model for understanding other cultural systems. . . . The function of language is to organize, to construct, indeed to provide us with our only access to reality.[64]

Thus, because language is how our reality is (re)presented and understood, any attempt at social change must begin with discourse. Changing the way people think about AIDS, which is determined by the language that is used to describe it, can be accomplished by challenging the signifying chain (created by biomedical discourse, and perpetuated by the government and the mass media) that not only links sex with sin with death, but also perpetuates the distinctions between the "innocent" and the "guilty victims" of AIDS.

The arguments of cultural critics like Patton and Treichler help us to understand why some AIDS activists have turned to performance as a means of intervening in the AIDS crisis. If, as these critics suggest, many of the damaging effects of the AIDS epidemic may be attributed to how it has been linguistically constructed, and if the dominant or mainstream discursive forms are indeed responsible for this construction, perhaps artistic or other cultural forms may provide vehicles for "deconstructing," "disfiguring," or "re-signifying" AIDS. From this perspective, performance would be an effective strategy of intervention insofar as it created new significations or representations that challenge the power/knowledge structure that disempowers people and creates communities that can act.

What is at issue in this position, of course, is the question of whether "success" or "effectiveness" can be construed in accordance with the views of these theorists. In other words, is it possible to argue that linguistic intervention in the dominant construction of AIDS will lead people to take an active role in the fight against AIDS? Will changing people's language inevitably lead to changes in behavior? Finally, is it possible to use performance in the deconstructive manner suggested by these theorists? In the chapters that follow, I focus on specific performances emerging out of the AIDS crisis in order to explore these questions. My purpose is not to provide definitive answers, but rather to examine both the possibilities and the limitations of this perspective. However, before discussing these performances, it is necessary to explain why performance is emerging as an important political tool in the contemporary or "postmodern" world according to performance theorists and how the intricacies of the performative act may assist in social change.

WHY PERFORMANCE?

In order to discuss the particularities related to performance as a particular art form, I begin by discussing the historical avant-garde and why its practitioners often selected performance as its method of choice. This discussion is followed by description of postmodern performance practices. I conclude this chapter by discussing the work of those involved with the anthropology of performance.

The historical avant-garde is a term often used to describe those early twentieth-century movements, such as Dadaism, Surrealism,

Expressionism, and Futurism, that arose as reactions to bourgeois art. In order to challenge bourgeois culture, the texts produced by the historical avant-garde attempted to break down the distinction between high and low art, between art and everyday life, and the notion of art as an institution.[65]

For many of these early movements, performance was the perfect tool to achieve their goals. As Rosa Lee Goldberg explains, "the Futurist painters turned to performance as the most direct means of forcing an audience to take note of their ideas."[66] She continues:

> Performance was the surest means of disrupting a complacent public. It gave artists licence [sic] to be both "creators" in developing a new form of artists' theatre, and "art objects" in that they made no separation between their art as poets, as painters or as performers.[67]

Thus, performance was the primary means through which the Futurists attempted to achieve their goals. In fact, in many of their manifestos, artists were encouraged to take their art into the streets, actions which often led to arrest.

Dadaism, another movement of the early twentieth century, also utilized performance, although performance was one of many forms chosen by the Dadaists. Started by Tristan Tzara in Switzerland in 1916, Dadaism was largely a reaction to World War I, which, the Dadaists argued, was a direct result of rational thinking and logic. As a result, the movement sought to replace logic and reason with chaos, and used its work to attack all institutions, such as science, religion, and art.

One performance-oriented event attributed to the Dadaists is the sound poem—poems not concerned with the meaning of words, but rather, the sounds of the vowels and consonants. Harriet Watts explains:

> Words "newly invented" and articulated in live performance were necessary to jar language loose from the mass-media grid where it is trapped in infinite commercial reproducibility. The word must be rendered unique, embodied and reenergized in unique human events that cannot be technically reproduced at will for unlimited mass consumption.[68]

Hence, performance was utilized because it, combined with the words used, was not reproducible, it was non-commodifiable. Everything rational was questioned by the Dadaists, and performance, they believed, was one medium through which such questioning could occur.

Performance played an integral role in each of the aforementioned movements. According to Goldberg, performance was a popular medium for the historical avant-garde because it was viewed as a way to break down categories and show new directions for artistic endeavors.[69] She further states that although much of what has been written about their work focuses on the "art objects produced by each period, it was more often than not the case that these movements found their roots and attempted to resolve problematic issues in performance."[70] More importantly, however, performance was viewed as a means through which these artists could achieve their goals. Goldberg argues that it "has been a way of appealing directly to a large public, as well as shocking audiences into reassessing their own notions of art and its relation to culture."[71] Similarly, Silvio Gaggi explains:

> When works of art enter the marketplace they are taken over by forces that have little to do with aesthetic value—whatever aesthetic value system one subscribes to. . . . Theatre and performance . . . produce unique works but do not produce permanent objects that can be owned. The movement of the visual artists into performance and conceptual modes can be seen as an attempt to avoid cooptation of the marketplace.[72]

Because the primary goals of each of these movements were to challenge the autonomy of the art object and the distinctions between "high" and "low" art, performance, according to Goldberg and Gaggi, was an obvious medium on which to rely. However, although the performance itself could not be coopted by the dominant culture, that is, it could not be bought and sold like a painting or sculpture, the techniques of these avant-garde movements (and subsequent performance practitioners attempting to challenge bourgeois values) have been coopted and depoliticized.

Although these movements died out prior to World War II, the impact of their ideas can be seen in various artistic endeavors occurring after the war. And although these experiments occurred in Europe, the influx of artists to the United States as a result of World War II had some impact, especially on performance.[73] Hence, what is referred to as the historical avant-garde did not really take hold in the United States, although it did influence a variety of artistic endeavors, especially after the war.

The influence of the historical avant-garde, as well as the theorists discussed in the previous section, can be found in postmodern performance practices. According to Andreas Huyssen, the historical avant-garde never took hold in the United States because "high art" was not as firmly established in the early 1920s as it was in Europe:

> Such an iconoclastic attack on cultural institutions and traditional modes of representation, narrative structure, perspective, and poetic sensibility [conducted by the historical avant-garde] only made sense in countries where "high art" had an essential role to play in legitimizing bourgeois political and social domination. . . . The cultural politics of the 20th-century avantgardism would have been meaningless (if not regressive) in the United States where "high art" was still struggling hard to gain wider legitimacy and to be taken seriously by the public.[74]

Hence, because the major goal of the historical avant-garde was to challenge the institution of bourgeois art, such attacks in the United States would have been irrelevant. In the 1950s, however, high art had established itself firmly within the culture of the United States. Because it had become institutionalized, the time was ripe for such challenges to emerge. And because the historical avant-garde was never acknowledged by the "Anglo-Saxon notions of modernism," events such as performance art and happenings appeared "more novel than they really were."[75]

Huyssen explains the link between the avant-garde movement in the United States and postmodernism, which, he argues, "was a product of the 1960s," by explaining how the postmodernism of the 1960s was not as radical as is often claimed.[76] He explains that although many claim that postmodernism suggests a radical break from tradition and the past, the resurgence of the historical avant-garde suggests a need for, rather than a rejection of, the avant-garde tradition. However, there are some differences between the historical avant-garde and postmodernism. For example, Huyssen states, "While postmodernism rebelled against the culture and politics of the 1950s, it nevertheless lacked a radical vision of social and political transformation that had been so essential to the historical avant-garde."[77] Additionally, as I suggested earlier, many of the techniques utilized to produce shock in the works of the historical avant-garde could no longer obtain such effects because the audiences of these postmodern texts "had been inculturated into modernism via the very same media."[78] Thus, the use of technology to shock the audiences of the early twentieth century did not have the same effect on audiences in the mid-1900s.

Postmodern forms of performance emerged during the late 1960s as a popular medium because, as Goldberg explains, it reduced "the element of alienation between performer and viewer—something that fitted well into the leftist inspiration of the investigation of the function of art—since both audience and performer experienced the work simultaneously."[79] These postmodern forms of performance often involved body art, living sculptures, autobiographies, and rituals.

Additionally, during this time a large number of performance groups appeared that dealt with issues specific to marginalized segments of the population. For women, gays, and other marginalized groups, an issue of primary importance was (and still is) representation; that is, challenging stereotypes that were part of their earlier representations in the theater by presenting alternative images of who they are.

In 1969, for example, feminist theatre groups arose around the country to address issues directly related to women.[80] Because they felt that theater was a "male entity,"[81] they began to experiment with other forms of performance (e.g., performance art), new spaces, and new audiences.[82] Dolan explains:

> The lighting, setting, costumes, blocking, text—all the material aspects of theatre—are manipulated so that the performance's meanings are intelligible to a particular spectator, constructed in a particular way by the terms of its address. Historically, in North American culture, this spectator has been assumed to be white, middle-class, heterosexual, and male.[83]

Not only were these theaters experimental in that most, if not all, of the audience members were women, but these performances also demand active participation from the audience.[84]

Performances such as these are examples of experiments that attempt to give voice to marginalized groups and to make them aware of their situation so that they can be capable of changing it. Some similarities can be drawn between feminist theatre groups and the performance experiments of Jerzy Grotowski and Augusto Boal in that they attempt to rethink agency by reconsidering the question of who speaks. Whereas the conventional theatrical frame essentially relegates the audience to a position of silent observer or witness to a self-enclosed dramatic universe, Grotowski and Boal attempt to challenge this frame.

Jerzy Grotowski's paratheater is one example of performance that challenges passivity ingrained in the audience by the conventional theatrical frame. Paratheater involves a reconceptualization of the audience so that there are no distinctions between performer and audience. During these performances a group may be taken into the woods for an extended period of time and "led through ritualized relivings of basic myths, archetypes, and symbols including fire, air, earth, water, eating, dancing, playing, planting, and bathing," the purpose of which is "to rediscover the roots of the theatre in pure ritualized experience, as well as to discover [one's] own true being."[85]

Similarly, the work of Augusto Boal also reflects an attempt to rethink agency in that it uses "ordinary people," as opposed to actors, as performers. In that sense, his performances, too, break down the traditional boundaries between actor and spectator. Like those working in feminist theatre, Boal also provides a voice for those who are often silenced—the working class. His particular goal is to make these people aware of their conditions so that they will be able to change them.

Instead of attempting to address a wider audience, feminist theatre, along with the work of Grotowski and Boal, addresses a smaller group of people. Each of these performance experiments serves to reconstitute the society to which the actor belongs. All are attempts to break down that artificial barrier between performers and spectators, and to give agency to those who are normally silenced.

But there are two problems with such attempts at reconceptualizing the role of the audience in order to promote social change. Particularly for Grotowski, the problem with this type of performance experiment is that it leads to a retreat from society rather than working within society to change it. Such a performance attempts to reimagine the social function of theater in a different way, the assumption being that by creating this kind of ritualistic experience, the "audience" will return to society with a transformed consciousness, which might, at some point, lead them to rethink the social structure. In other words, the performance postpones social change to some indefinite time in the future. Similarly, in regards to Boal, it could be argued that although the specific intent of his work is to open the eyes of the lower classes to their oppression and give them ways to challenge it, like Grotowski, his theater also postpones social change to some indefinite time in the future.[86]

Elizabeth Burns raises another issue related to audience participation. She states, "When the spectators themselves are expected to take part the outer edges of the theatrical world dissolve."[87] However, she also maintains that such an attempt is difficult for audience members because they expect to "cast off their social roles, to remain passive and unpresented."[88] Burns argues that even when audience members are asked to participate, they are actually being props for actors. In this case, the audience members are neither part of the performance nor totally detached from it—they are in a liminal state between their real existence and the fictional world of the play. And in some ways this liminal state is not very different from their ordinary role as spectator. So if Burns is correct in suggesting that when people participate in the performance, they view themselves as part of the performance instead of viewing the performance as part of their lives, such experimentation with audience participation may be ineffectual.

Returning to the example of feminist theatre, it may be that the most successful efforts along these lines are those occasions where feminist theatre seems to emerge as a kind of consciousness raising. According to Natalle, feminist theatre aligns itself with the strategies of the feminist movement in that it serves a consciousness-raising function. The performances of Augusto Boal serve this same function. That is, they make members of the working class aware of the structures that confine and silence them, thereby providing them with or the opportunity for agency—something, as I have argued, some mainstream theater performances fail to provide.

The question of who gets to speak, of having different voices being heard, of giving agency, brings us to cultural studies—particularly its position on experience as a potentially critical category. According to Raymond Williams, there are certain "structures of feeling" and experience that are normally silenced in the most popular or mainstream art forms. And from this perspective, what we have to consider is that even a classic realist playwright like Ibsen or Chekhov could be considered "revolutionary" to the extent that they placed on stage virtually for the first time in the history of theater ordinary, middle-class citizens and their own domestic problems. Prior to this, most playwrights ignored issues related to these people, choosing instead to present the lives of the upper-classes and royalty. It is conceivable, then, that a classic realist playwright today could serve a consciousness-raising function similar to the experiments of Boal and Grotowski, thereby enhancing the potential for social change.

In addition to the question of who speaks, there is a theoretical reconsideration of performance and agency that emerges in light of postmodernism's privileging of irony and parody, an issue addressed by Bowman and Pollock in relation to Pina Bausch's *Tanztheater*. Pollock explains that Bausch's *Tanztheater* emerged from "a movement that began in the 1960s, in large part out of frustration with the classical ballet techniques and hierarchies that had dominated East and West Germany since World War II."[89] Bowman and Pollock argue that Bausch's work reflects how "the body as subject is repressed."[90] However, in her work the body also challenges this position. They explain, "in the interstices of the performed text and the social text we see—feel—the possibility for social change: not for doing away with the social text but for rewriting it." Finally, they explain how this work shows that although the woman's body, which is often presented as passive, "is not 'naturally' passive."[91] In a more general sense, what Bowman and Pollock seem to argue is that enacting a particular subject position self-consciously can restore agency to those who lack agency. Within such enactment lies the potential for social change.

The work of many performance artists also appears to rely on a belief that agency can be restored by enacting a pre-written text self-consciously. Like the performances created by Pina Bausch, Karen Finley is one performance artist whose work reflects these assumptions. In her work, Finley often performs subject positions that are degrading to women. By enacting her status of a second-class citizen and challenging this position through a self-conscious performance, she restores agency to herself. Her performance, in its self-consciousness, rearticulates pre-given texts or languages and, it could be argued, provides the potential for social change. For, like Pina Bausch's performances, Finley shows how the body "can escape neither its social determinations nor its objective materiality." As a result, the hope for social change lies not in the performance process alone, "but in the alterative power of the performed body: in finding the 'strength' to exert the signifying power of the body over and against—but without denying—its social insignia."[92] As in Bausch's work, by both accepting and simultaneously rejecting a particular subject position, Finley's performance has the potential for social change.

In summary, many postmodern performance practices suggest that the self-consciousness inherent in these performances prevents both the performer and the audience from being interpolated by their positions as subject. In contrast to reflexive experiments that were largely formal or text-based, in many postmodern forms of performance the performers are aware of their subject positions and use this awareness to create a new awareness in their audiences. The performer, from this perspective, has agency. And while these performers may utilize formal experiments, most do not assume that the incorporation of these experiments is the means through which social change will occur. Instead, in many forms of postmodern performance we find a reliance on realism, which, as Jameson argues, may be the most effective means of subversion.[93]

A final perspective on "why performance" is found in the work of performance anthropologists. This perspective argues that performance is culture-specific, that both its forms and functions cannot be specified in advance. Instead, performance must be viewed as part of a culture's entire system of communication. Such a redefinition of performance challenges some other conceptions of art and performance by drawing attention to its own cultural specificity—its own constructedness. To a certain extent, cross-cultural studies of performance have relativized our own performance categories; that is, they have made us aware that our own distinctions between "performance" and "not-performance," or "good" performance and "bad" performance, are neither natural nor necessary, but matters of value-governed choice.

This perspective is often linked to the work of sociologists, such as Erving Goffman, who have drawn our attention to theatricality of everyday life—that the distinctions between "acting" and "behaving" are not so clear cut. And, of course, the theatrum mundi metaphor—that "All the world is a stage"—has been with us for centuries. One critique of this sociological view has been that the "life is theater" perspective often is determined by the person studying the behavior, not the people engaging in the behavior.[94] In other words, the people actually doing the "acting" or "role playing" are unreflective or unanalytical about what they are doing.

Those interested in the anthropology of performance seek to supplement the insights of dramaturgical social theorists like Goffman by showing how social actors do demonstrate a reflexive awareness of the theatricality of everyday life. From this perspective, performance is not a category imposed on all social behavior-in-general; neither is it a term for routinized or patterned behavior; instead, it is a more specific, even special, category that emerges in relation to a culture's entire system of communication.[95] Comparing his work to Goffman's, Victor Turner suggests that if life is theater, than performance "is a kind of metatheatre, a dramaturgical language about the language of ordinary role-playing and status-maintenance which constitutes communication in the quotidian social process."[96] While some view performance as a secondary, peripheral, or even parasitic form of speech and behavior in relation to ordinary or instrumental communication, performance anthropologists see it rather as constitutive of other forms and functions of communication. Performances, Victor Turner argues:

> are not simple reflectors or expressions of culture or even of
> changing culture but may themselves be *active agencies of change*,
> representing the eye by which culture sees itself and the drawing
> board on which creative actors sketch out what they believe to be
> more apt or interesting "designs for living."[97]

For Turner, then, performance is both a reflective and a
reflexive act. It not only responds to the culture, but also has the
potential to produce, to resist, to change the culture in which the
performance occurs. Thus, because performance is viewed as both a
reflective and reflexive act, from this perspective the relationship
between performance as a cultural form or position and society is
considered highly unstable—perhaps uniquely so in relation to other
cultural forms.

Turner believes that the public reflexivity experienced in
performance is an experience of openness or unfinishedness in the social
world. Everyday social categories, structures, or systems are revealed
not as fixed or stable, but as fluid, unstable, and emergent. As a result,
every performance is both a means of re-viewing the social text and
potentially a means of rewriting it. However, this view does not mean
that every performance is revolutionary; instead, it means that within
every performance is the potential for producing social change.

Much of Turner's work is concerned with rites of passage.
These rites go through three stages: separation, transition, and
reintegration. Separation involves the separation of "secular space" from
"sacred space" and involves symbolic behavior in which the "ritual
subjects" are detached "from their previous social statuses."[98] The
transition stage involves liminality, "a period and area of ambiguity."
Reintegration involves the return of the ritual subjects to their society.
Turner's discussion of ritual and rites of passage suggests that
performance is both structural and anti-structural. That is, even though
the ritual process is often employed as a conservative mechanism, as a
means to reinforce the social order, the experience of liminality is anti-
structural and therefore outside the bounds of the social system. While
this experience of liminality is often meant to terrorize the initiate in a
ritual, the communitas that often develops during those moments of
liminality is an experience that ritual subjects sometimes learn to enjoy.

As Jeffrey Alexander explains, from Turner's perspective, "Liminality can be an incitement to action and social change, as it is in millennial movements, either communist or religious, or in the defiant activities of marginal groups like beatniks, hippies, and punks."[99]

While Turner's work originates from a study of ritual and focuses predominantly on pre-industrial societies, Richard Schechner has applied Turner's insights to what he calls "ordinary theatre."[100] In *Between Theatre and Anthropology*, Schechner suggests that the strength and efficacy of performance lies in its duplicity, the liminality inherent in the performance act. As Schechner explains, during the performance, the actor

> performs in the field between a negative and a double negative, a field of limitless potential, free as it is from both the person (not) and the person impersonated (not not). All effective performances share this "not-not not" quality: Olivier is not Hamlet, but also he is not not Hamlet: his performance is between a denial of being another (= I am me) and a denial of not being another (= I am Hamlet).[101]

Not only is liminality part of the actor's experience, it is also found in the performance itself. The audience members experience liminality during a performance because they are neither part of the performance nor totally detached from it—they are in a liminal state between their real existence and the fictional world of the performance. Again, this duplicity is one element that empowers the performance act. Other qualities of performance, discussed below, also exhibit this duplicitous nature.

Schechner distinguishes between performances that are transportational and those that are transformational. Transportational performances, he argues, are performances in which "the performers are 'taken somewhere' but at the end, often assisted by others, they are 'cooled down' and reenter ordinary life just about where they went in."[102] Transformational performances are those that result in some kind of lasting change in the performer. Both types of performances, he suggests, work together in that "a series of transportation performances can achieve a transformation."[103] He further asserts that while most people view transportation performances as theater and transformation performances as rituals, both types of performance exist in any event.[104]

The aforementioned information applies specifically to the performers, not the audience. But Schechner does discuss the audience in relation to each of these performances; however, here he distinguishes between these two types. For transformational performances, the audience usually wants the performance to succeed. As in a ritual, the audience is often comprised of members of the performer's family and/or community. Also, Schechner notes, the performer in this situation may not be the most technically adept at his/her task. In transportational performances, on the other hand, the performer's skill is important, and, in some cases, his/her status is even more important than his/her performance skills.[105]

As a result of this information, Schechner derives four variables he believes operate in every performance. The first variable involves the efficacious versus fictive nature of the performance, similar to a distinction he has made elsewhere between efficacy and entertainment, each of which forms opposite ends of a continuum. Efficacious performances, closely linked to rituals, intend to be transformative; entertaining performances are linked to theater. However, Schechner argues "[n]o performance is pure efficacy or pure entertainment."[106]

In addition to presenting characteristics of each of these categories, he includes examples of each of these performances as they have been found in western theater since the 1500s. In modern times, examples of efficacious performances include Jerzy Grotowski's paratheater, experimental performance, political theater, and performative psychotherapies; examples of entertaining performances include commercial theater, regional theater, theme parks, and street entertainers.[107] Schechner further explains that efficacy was dominant in the 1960s and 1970s (arguably attributable to the political climate), and was replaced by an emphasis on entertainment in the 1980s.[108]

The other variables inherent in a performance event include "the status of the roles within a performance," "the status of the persons playing the roles,"[109] and "the quality of the performance," determined by how well the performers have mastered the skills demanded.[110] He concludes that all of these variables are present in all performances, transformational or transportational.

Schechner believes the future for theater lies in the work of anthropologists and performance specialists. These people, he argues, provide us with an expanded view of what constitutes performance:

> of how ritual and popular and artistic performances affect people, and what functions performance might fulfill across a broad spectrum including entertainment, social action, education, and healing. Concepts of shamanism, performance theory, and social drama have joined my earlier awareness of orthodox and experimental theater.[111]

Thus, for Schechner, attention to other forms of performance is essential.

What the analysis in this section suggests is that to decipher the political rhetoric of AIDS performances we need to adopt the fullest possible view of performance and a broad understanding of its potential. As we have seen, it is impossible to predict that a radical social role for the theater will develop from formal experimentation. Nor can we deny that a significant social change might result from even the most conventional forms of theater. Instead, to paraphrase Shapiro, we must focus our attention on the individual performance's tendency to reproduce dominant forms of discourse or provoke critical analysis.[112] In this sense, a performance plays a politically radical social role when it opens up questions of power and authority, questions which are sometimes, but not always, silenced by conventional theatrical forms.

PREVIEW AND LIMITATIONS

The following chapters are divided according to the various forms performances have taken. In each, I describe various texts and performances, how they were received, and their effectiveness for social change. Chapter 2 focuses on two conventional theatrical performances—*As Is* and *The Normal Heart*. Chapter 3 focuses on performance artists Karen Finley and Tim Miller and discusses the effectiveness of this more recent, alternative form of performance.

Chapter 4 analyzes three cultural performances, two of which were sponsored by ACT-UP (AIDS Coalition to Unleash Power), and The NAMES Project (AIDS Memorial Quilt). The final chapter summarizes the study and draws some conclusions regarding the efficacy of performance for social change, particularly from the perspective of these cultural theorists.

In order to limit the scope of this study, seven performances emerging out of the AIDS crisis will be discussed. It cannot be argued that these performances are either "representative" or the "best" performances arising out of the crisis. Instead, they were selected based on their familiarity, which resulted from the amount of press received. Except for ACT-UP's "Condom Day," each of these performances received widespread attention in the popular media, and can be compared and contrasted for their effectiveness in intervening in the AIDS crisis. The lack of attention afforded "Condom Day" provides additional insight into the way the dominant culture handles information that is not in line with its ideology.

An additional limitation involves the nature of the AIDS texts discussed. This study focuses solely on live performance, since bringing in film and television, for example, would have required a discussion of issues unique to those media as they are distinguished from live performance events. However, the role the mass media plays in disseminating information about these live performances is crucial when discussing the responses to these performances, as well as their effectiveness for intervening in the AIDS crisis.

One final limitation refers to the location of these performances. Although a number of AIDS-related performances have been witnessed throughout the world, all the performances described in this study occurred in the United States (although some also have been presented abroad). This decision was made for two reasons. The first reason is largely pragmatic: performances are difficult to document and information about them is hard to come by; these difficulties would be compounded if I chose to extend the scope of this study to other countries. The second reason is theoretical: as each performance must be viewed in the context in which it occurs, performances in other countries cannot be studied without bringing in issues of how the AIDS crisis has evolved in that particular country. As Watney notes:

> It is always important to recognize that every country affected by HIV has its own epidemic, shaped by the local circumstances of the population groups in which the virus first emerges. This is not to say that HIV is a different disease in different countries, but that the patterns of its transmission are profoundly influenced by social context.[113]

Since my primary emphasis is on how these various forms of performance attempt to intervene in the AIDS crisis in the United States, drawing such comparisons between countries is not of primary importance to this study.

SCOPE AND SIGNIFICANCE

Support for this project lies in its unique approach to studying both performances attempting to intervene in the AIDS crisis as well as the use of performance as a vehicle for social change. First, although a number of researchers have considered the efficacy of performance for social change, many of these studies are limited by their analysis of the conventional theatrical form.[114] Second, while a number of recent studies have looked at the political implications of non-conventional performance, comparisons between conventional and non-conventional performances are lacking.[115] Third, most critical/cultural studies focus on texts presented on television and film. Considerably less research has been conducted on live performances either in the traditional or expanded definition of the term.[116] Fourth, this study attempts to explain the various, but related, issues that determine how these cultural events relate to and affect society. Finally, this study provides those involved in the AIDS crisis with an understanding of whether performance can be used to intervene discursively in the dominant construction of AIDS, and, more importantly, if discursive intervention is an effective strategy for promoting social change.

NOTES

1. Stallybrass and White, 80.

2. The first article related to what is now called AIDS actually appeared in *Morbidity and Mortality Weekly Report*, a publication by the Center for Disease Control, on June 5, 1981. *The New York Times* is credited with the first press report.

3. The most recent HIV/AIDS statistics can obtained by calling the Center for Disease Control's National AIDS Clearinghouse.

4. Treichler, "Contests for Meaning" 229.

5. Treichler, "Contests for Meaning" 232.

6. Watney, "AIDS" 184.

7. Wallis xv.

8. Shapiro 130.

9. For example, in his 1991 article, Radetsky suggests that the first person with AIDS-like symptoms died in 1959.

10. Altman 21.

11. Gilman 89.

12. Altman 33.

13. It should be noted here that AIDS is not a disease. Besides the obvious fact that "Acquired Immune Deficiency Syndrome *disease*" makes no sense linguistically (although it is most often referred to as such), the use of the word "disease" has serious ramifications. From a purely medical standpoint, Watney argues, AIDS is comprised of many "distinct diseases, tumours [sic], cancers, and so on, which may occur in many different combinations and sequences in the wake of HIV infection and damage to the body's immunological defences [sic]" ("Taking Liberties" 15). He also asserts that while "HIV is infectious in a limited number of circumstances," AIDS "is neither infectious nor contagious, since its various symptoms are direct results of previous HIV infection" ("AIDS" 184).

14. "At risk" categories imply that persons who are not members of a certain group are safe from AIDS. However, as Watney notes, "With HIV it cannot be sufficiently emphasized that risk comes from what you do, not how you label yourself. There is no *intrinsic* relation between HIV and any individual or population" ("AIDS" 185).

15. Falwell's quote is cited in Crimp ("Cultural Analysis" 8). Like male homosexuals, the other groups most heavily affected by AIDS are also marginalized by society. As Larry Kramer explains, the reason for complacency about AIDS is unquestionably a result of "who it's happening to. . . . [T]his is happening to black people and to Hispanic people and to people who take drugs and to gay people and to babies who are born out of wedlock, and these are all people that a lot of other people" wish were not here (Interview 8).

16. Altman 24-25.

17. Shilts xxi.

18. Shilts 578.

19. Patton 114.

20. Watney, "Taking Liberties" 18.

21. Information on the Stonewall riot was obtained from D'Emilio (*Sexual Politics* 231-33). D'Emilio's data were derived from newspaper reports appearing after the riot.

22. D'Emilio, *Sexual Politics* 232.

23. D'Emilio, *Sexual Politics* 233.

24. Altman 14.

25. Altman 24.

26. Altman 39.

27. Altman 39.

28. Williamson 79.

29. Williamson 70.

30. Gilman 90.

31. Gilman 89-90.

32. Poovey 621.

33. Many writing about the government's slow response to the AIDS crisis compare it to other health crises, particularly the outbreak of Legionnaires' Disease in 1976 and the Tylenol Scare of 1982, and argue that because these potential epidemics did not occur in an already marginalized group, the government and medical institutions were quick to intervene (see, e.g., Kramer, *Reports*; Altman; Shilts). The Tylenol crisis, which occurred during the early stages of the AIDS epidemic, serves as an excellent point of comparison. As Shilts explains the Tylenol scare "showed how the government could spring into action,

issue warnings, change regulations, and spend money, lots of money, when they thought the lives of Americans were at stake" (191).

34. Watney, *Policing* 11.
35. Patton 18.
36. Patton 16.
37. Patton 18.
38. Patton 19.
39. Patton 20.
40. Grover 29-30.
41. Grover 29.
42. Qtd. in Patton 136.
43. Patton 57.
44. Patton 57.
45. Treichler, "How to Have Theory" 97.
46. Treichler 71.
47. Treichler 69-70.
48. Gallagher 32.
49. Watney, "Taking Liberties" 33.
50. Gallagher 33.
51. Gallagher 32.
52. Ehrenfeld 10.
53. Callahan 82.
54. "Martina" A1.
55. These articles are by Elson and Swift, respectively.
56. Although it is estimated that three-fourths of all persons with HIV/AIDS in the world are heterosexual, the number of heterosexuals in the United States is not nearly as high.
57. Altman 23.
58. Patton 4.
59. Patton 124-25.
60. Stallybrass and White, 80.
61. Patton 125.
62. Treichler, "AIDS, Homophobia" 31.
63. Treichler, "AIDS, Homophobia" 32.
64. G. Turner 13.
65. Huyssen 163.

66. Goldberg 14. Futurism was the first avant-garde movement. Beginning in Paris in 1909, this movement sought to reject the past and transform humankind. Rather than rejecting technology, the Futurists used technological advances to their benefit. In fact, they used technology as the basis of their art. Also, rather than using conventional spaces for performances and exhibitions, the Futurists utilized nightclubs, music halls, circuses, the streets, and other non-traditional spaces to present their works. For additional information on this movement, as well as others, see Goldberg.

67. Goldberg 15-16.

68. Watts 123.

69. Goldberg 7.

70. Goldberg 7-8.

71. Goldberg 8.

72. Gaggi 78.

73. Goldberg 121.

74. Huyssen 167.

75. Huyssen 166-67.

76. Huyssen 168.

77. Huyssen 169.

78. Huyssen 170.

79. Goldberg 152.

80. Natalle 13.

81. Bassnett-McGuire, ctd. in Bennett 61.

82. Bennett 62.

83. Dolan 1.

84. For a discussion of feminist theatre in the United States, see Natalle. In this book she provides a history of feminist theatre and provides a detailed description of a number of plays that have been produced by various feminist theatre groups throughout the United States. A more thorough (and I would argue insightful) discussion of the relationship between feminism and theatre, performance, popular culture, and literature is found in Jill Dolan's *The Feminist Spectator as Critic*. Not only does she clearly explain how feminist performers and audiences deal with issues of representation, she also focuses attention on how critics deal with feminist performances.

85. Brockett 696.

86. I am not arguing that future action does not constitute social change. Instead, I am suggesting that the reliance on some indefinite future action is a criticism that has been leveled against this particular approach to performance and social change.

87. Burns 49.

88. Burns 40.

89. Pollock 97.

90. Bowman and Pollock 116.

91. Bowman and Pollock 117.

92. Bowman and Pollock 115.

93. Jameson 146.

94. See, e.g., Messinger et al.

95. This perspective is based on the work of Dell Hymes and is cited in Fine and Speer.

96. V. Turner, *Anthropology* 76.

97. V. Turner, *Anthropology* 24 (emphasis added).

98. V. Turner, *From Ritual* 24.

99. Alexander 20.

100. Schechner, *Performance Theory* 252-253.

101. Schechner, *Between* 123.

102. Schechner, *Between* 125-26.

103. Schechner, *Between* 126.

104. Schechner, *Between* 130.

105. Schechner, *Between* 132.

106. Schechner, *Performance Theory* 120.

107. Schechner, *Performance Theory* 122.

108. Schechner, *Performance Theory* 122.

109. Schechner explains that this variable refers to whether or not the individuals are "playing themselves (as in initiations), are possessed by others, or have . . . built a role" (*Between* 133).

110. Schechner, *Between* 133.

111. Schechner, *End* 72.

112. Shapiro 130.

113. Watney, "AIDS" 186.

114. Some examples include Hermassi's study of Greek, Elizabethan, and contemporary theater, Levine's study of left-wing theater in America, and Natalle's study of feminist theatre as persuasion.

115. See, e.g., Kepke and Shields.

116. One notable exception is Susan Bennett's *Theatre Audiences*, which uses cultural studies as a means to explore the relationship between the performance event and audience response. However, while she discusses the work of Schechner, Turner, and others, her study takes as its primary emphasis performances occurring in the traditional theater space. In fact, she uses their work as a justification for studying the audience.

II

Conventional Theater

As Is and *The Normal Heart*

> Compared to television's live coverage every night of the latest
> election campaign or hostage crisis, theater may seem like a
> cumbersome form of communication, lagging years behind in
> dealing with the urgent issues of the day. Yet theater can often
> lead, asserting its ancient function as a public forum in which a
> community gathers to talk about itself. The best contemporary
> example is the theater's response to the AIDS crisis.[1]

One of the primary problems facing AIDS plays is how to
achieve a balance between art and politics. In other words, in order for
plays about AIDS to make it to and survive in mainstream theaters, they
must conform to certain audience expectations without compromising
their political agenda. While Shewey's introductory comment reflects a
rather general and optimistic view of AIDS plays in regards to a
specific political function, it fails to recognize that such a tension exists;
that is, he ignores the question of whether the mainstream theater
"forum" enables the kind of talk that can lead to social change.

This tension, reflected in mainstream AIDS plays, is not far
removed from the tensions experienced by other gay plays attempting
to make it in conventional theaters. As Mark Gevisser explains:

> [J]ust as black culture has been presented to mainstream white
> America as a minstrel show. . ., gay culture is presented to
> mainstream heterosexual America as a drag show. [Plays such as
> *Torch Song Trilogy, La Cage Aux Folles*, and *M. Butterfly*] present
> startling images to conservative Broadway houses, but the reason
> they have done so well is precisely because they *do* present

startling images. They are spectacles that . . . exploit homosexuality
as the kind of exotic entertainment red-blooded Americans would
enjoy on a night out in the city.
And their conventional theatrical forms render them safe
and unthreatening.[2]

Thus, according to Gevisser, the success of these plays in mainstream theaters is linked to their exploitative representations of gay culture. As long as they exploit homosexuality to entertain their audiences, gay plays succeed on Broadway. Furthermore, the closer gay plays move to Broadway audiences, the more they have to conform to specific standards of the mainstream dramatic form; the greater their distance from Broadway, the more able they are to speak to specific reading communities without compromising their political agenda.

The plays mentioned by Gevisser, *Torch Song Trilogy, M. Butterfly*, and *La Cage Aux Folles*, are "pre-AIDS" plays. They are representative of the type of gay plays that achieved mainstream success prior to the AIDS crisis and serve as a point of comparison for those plays presented during the crisis. Additionally, these plays often appear to compromise the political for the aesthetic or entertainment value endemic to conventional or mainstream theater. For if they had challenged the audience to reconceive their notions of homosexuality, they probably would not have made it to Broadway.

The purpose of this chapter is to explore how the tension between art and politics manifests itself and is handled in two mainstream plays occurring during the AIDS crisis, William M. Hoffman's *As Is* and Larry Kramer's *The Normal Heart*, and to discuss the effectiveness of this particular form of performance for social change. I am concerned with how these plays, occurring within the context of the AIDS crisis, create a balance between art and politics. The central issue I examine is whether the popularity of these plays, together with their presentation in mainstream theaters, affected the impact of their political message.

The two plays were selected for a number of reasons. First, they are arguably two of the most popular plays that have emerged out of the AIDS crisis. Not only are these plays still performed in the United States, they have both been produced in a number of countries throughout the world. Second, because both appeared at approximately the same time, they are part of the same cultural/historical "moment" in the AIDS crisis. They were also two of the first plays about AIDS created. Third, although both plays are performed in mainstream theaters, each play takes a different approach to the AIDS issue.

To explore the balance between art and politics in the plays, I begin by presenting a brief plot summary of each of these plays, followed by a discussion of the similarities and differences between them at the level of the dramatic text. Second, I compare the critical responses to each of these plays based on the criteria through which they were judged. Finally, I discuss the effectiveness of this particular form of performance for social change. Specifically, I will be concerned with how Hoffman and Kramer attempt to balance aesthetics and politics in their plays, and how attempting to achieve such a balance affects their ability to have a social impact.

THE TEXTS

William M. Hoffman's *As Is* officially opened at the Circle Repertory Company (CRC) in New York City on March 10, 1985. On May 1, 1985, the play moved to Broadway's Lyceum Theatre and proceeded to win a number of awards, including a Drama Desk Award and an Obie Award; it also received three Tony nominations. Larry Kramer's *The Normal Heart* opened on April 21, 1985, at Joseph Papp's Public Theater as part of the New York Shakespeare Festival. While the play never moved to Broadway and did not receive the critical acclaim evidenced in the awards given to *As Is*, *The Normal Heart* does have the distinction of being the longest running show in the history of the Public Theater and it was nominated for an Olivier award in London.

The plot of *As Is* centers around a relationship between Rich, who has just been diagnosed with AIDS, and Saul, his former lover, and the effect that AIDS has on their relationship and their lives. However, the play is not a linear narrative that centers solely on this relationship. The play also shows the impact that AIDS has had on the lives of those other than Rich and Saul, with whom Rich has interacted (e.g., doctors, hospice workers, friends, family) and on others who have been diagnosed with the virus. These scenes do not occur in chronological order. Some of the scenes are clearly flashbacks, but it is often difficult to discern whether a given scene occurred in the fictive past, is in the fictive present, or will occur in the future. Regardless, it is through these scenes that we learn the impact that AIDS has had on people. All these other characters in the play are portrayed by members of a chorus.

While *As Is* uses a personal approach to the AIDS issue by focusing primarily on the relationship between Rich and Saul, *The Normal Heart* is an autobiographical and overtly political text. The plot centers around Ned Weeks (the alter-ego of Larry Kramer) and his conflict with the Gay Men's Health Crisis (GMHC), which Weeks, one of the founders of the group, believes is not handling the crisis properly because it refuses to tell gay men to stop having sex.[3] Throughout the play, Weeks also condemns other dominant institutions for their indifference to the crisis.

A number of similarities and differences exist between these two plays at the level of the dramatic text. These points of comparison include: (1) how the AIDS issue is handled and what we learn about the virus; (2) how the plays are categorized; (3) the status of persons represented; and (4) the incorporation of Brechtian alienation techniques.

The first and most obvious similarity between these two plays is that they are dealing with AIDS. And, as Clive Barnes argues, both plays

> . . . are politically slanted, in that they wish to awaken awareness
> of this menace to society, and to ensure that adequate measures,
> particularly money for urgent, desperately needed research, are
> taken, and that the growing horror of this plague receives its proper
> awareness.[4]

However, as the plot summaries indicate, each play takes a unique approach to the AIDS issue. *The Normal Heart* is overtly political, while *As Is* is more personal. The former addresses the politics surrounding the AIDS crisis and explicitly condemns the government, the media, and the gay community itself for not working harder to draw attention to the virus and to obtain resources to deal with it. The effect that the virus has on individuals is not as prominent an issue as it seems to be in *As Is*. In fact, it is probably the overt political nature of the play, as well as its tone, that led fourteen agents to refuse Kramer's play before Papp agreed to produce it.[5]

When the personal impact of AIDS is mentioned in *The Normal Heart*, it only serves to support the larger theme of the play. One such example occurs near the end of the play in a scene between Bruce and Ned. Bruce, a vice-president for a large, New York bank who is not openly gay, is the person elected by the group to be the president of the newly-formed organization. Prior to this scene, most of the interactions between Bruce and Ned are conflicts over Bruce's handling of the organization. In the scene, Bruce explains what happened to his lover, Albert, immediately prior to and after Albert's death:

> . . . [Albert's] mother wanted him back in Phoenix before he died, this was last week when it was obvious, so I get permission from Emma and bundle him all up and take him to the plane in an ambulance. The pilot wouldn't take off and I refused to leave the plane . . . so finally they get another pilot. . . . And when we got to Phoenix, there's a police van waiting for us and all the police are in complete protective rubber clothing.[6]

By the time Bruce and Albert arrived at the hospital, Albert has died. Bruce continues his monologue by telling Ned that the doctors would not examine Albert's body. As a result, there was no death certificate, and so neither the police nor the undertakers would collect the body. Bruce ends his monologue by explaining:

> Finally, some orderly comes in and stuffs Albert in a heavy-duty Glad Bag and motions us with his finger to follow and he puts him out in the back alley with the garbage. He says, "Hey, man. See what a big favor I've done for you, I got him out, I want fifty bucks." I paid him and then his mother and I carried the bag to her car and we finally found a black undertaker who cremated him for a thousand dollars, no questions asked.[7]

In addition to this scene, several other scenes between Ned and Felix illustrate the impact that the epidemic is having on individuals; however, all these scenes serve to support the larger political agenda of the play—that nothing is being done about AIDS. In *As Is*, on the other hand, the virus is dealt with on a more personal level. The plot of the play centers around the effect of Rich's infection on Saul's life and their relationship as a whole. As Hoffman said, "I didn't write the play to inform people about AIDS. . . . My play is about people and what happens when tragedy strikes their lives."[8] Similarly, Kramer argues that his intention in writing *The Normal Heart* was not only to inform people about AIDS. He says he "wrote it to be a love story, in honor of a man I loved who died. . . . I wanted people to see that gay men in love and gay men suffering and gay men dying are just like everyone else."[9]

Still, it is important to discuss what these plays say about AIDS and persons with AIDS (PWAs), and to see exactly what each of these plays attempts to tell us about the virus and its impact. While Hoffman's avowed intention was for the relationship between the two men to be foregrounded, throughout the play we do get a great deal of information about the virus. We find out the symptoms, the causes, possible treatments, and, sometimes, we are shown how PWAs are treated by various people in society. For example, at the end of the play, during a scene between Rich and his brother, we find out that AIDS cannot be transmitted through casual contact. When his brother enters his hospital room wearing a surgical gown, mask, and gloves, Rich tells him, "Unless you're planning to come into intimate contact with me or my body fluids, none of that shit you have on is necessary." When the brother begins to explain that he put on these clothes because of the sign on the door, Rich says, "But please restrain your brotherly affection for my sake; who knows what diseases you might have brought in with you?"[10]

This scene presents us with two facts about AIDS. First, we find out that it is transmitted through an exchange of body fluids. Second, we learn that persons who do not have AIDS are a danger to persons with AIDS. Although the play does not belabor this point, Rich's aforementioned comment refers to the fact that because a PWA's immune system is so weak, any contact with a person who is ill (e.g., has a cold or the flu) can have a devastating effect on those with AIDS because their bodies do not have the ability to fight an infection.

In *As Is*, we also find out that AIDS has moved into the heterosexual community; however, because this revelation overlaps with a conversation between Rich and his doctors, it may be missed by the audience. Similarly, the doctors provide some information about AIDS. But due to the context in which this exchange occurs and the lack of credibility that seems to be afforded the doctors in the play, this information is likely to be ignored by audience members. For example, one of the doctors tells Rich what AIDS is by declaring, "Your suppressor cells outnumber your helper cells."[11] This information, while accurate, is so technical that it serves to confuse Rich (and perhaps the audience) about the nature of AIDS. In addition, this statement is presented during a scene where Rich's friends and family are responding to his disclosure that he has AIDS. Because some of their dialogue overlaps with what the doctors are telling Rich, it is likely that some, if not all, of the information about AIDS will fail to reach the audience.

Finally, in *As Is* we are also shown how PWAs are treated. When Rich attempts to pick up a man at a bar and tells him that he has AIDS, the person, who had expressed interest, says, "No way. Uh-uh . . . . Good luck . . . . Oh, man. . . ."[12] Another scene that is particularly informative involves members of the chorus (playing the roles of Chet, Lily, Rich's brother, various doctors, and Rich's business partner). Here we discover that Chet wants to leave Rich, that Rich's brother refused to use the bathroom at Rich's house, and that he is worried about his children. At the end of this scene, in what is probably one of the more hard-hitting moments in the play, Rich attempts to put his arm around Chet and, in unison, all these characters (except Saul) say, "Don't touch me!" and back off "terrified."[13]

In *The Normal Heart* we also learn information about AIDS, although the term is never used. First, as in *As Is*, we find out how PWAs are treated. In *The Normal Heart*, though, institutions, as opposed to individuals, are indicted for their mistreatment of PWAs.

When Dr. Emma Brookner, the person who initially persuaded Ned to tell gay men to stop having sex, is denied funding for research, she denounces the medical community for its self-centered economics:

> How does it always happen that all the idiots are always on your team? You guys have all the money, call the shots, shut everybody out, and then operate behind closed doors. I am taking care of more victims of this epidemic than anyone in the world. We have more accumulated test results, more data, more frozen blood samples, more experience! How can you not fund my research or invite me to participate in yours? A promising virus has already been discovered—in France. Why are we being told not to cooperate with the French? Just so you can steal a Nobel Prize?[14]

On a more personal level, Bruce's monologue about his lover's death (described earlier) also provides a disturbing and illuminating example about how people in the medical community feel about PWAs.

In addition to indicting the medical community, Kramer's play also attacks the government for its inactivity, and thus further explains how PWAs are treated. The government is indicted most adamantly by Ned, but also by Dr. Brookner. She is the one who introduces the problem to Ned and explains the inactivity on the part of both the government and the medical community. When Ned asks why nothing has been done about the "disease," even though it has been around for more than a year, Brookner replies:

> They know about it. You have a Commissioner of Health who got burned with the Swine Flu epidemic, declaring an epidemic when there wasn't one. The government appropriated $150 million for that mistake. You have a Mayor who's a bachelor and I assume afraid of being perceived as too friendly to anyone gay. And who is also out to protect a billion-dollar-a-year tourist industry. He's not about to tell the world there's an epidemic menacing his city. And don't ask me about the President.[15]

All these examples provide us with information about how the AIDS virus was handled in the early years and how persons with AIDS were treated.

The Normal Heart also informs us about the symptoms and supposed causes of AIDS, predominantly from Dr. Brookner. Unlike the doctors in *As Is*, her voice gets heard by the audience. She is a credible source (and sympathetic, given the fact that she is in a wheelchair), and therefore what she says is heard by both Weeks and the audience when she tells us what AIDS is. Also, as opposed to the doctors in *As Is*, Brookner uses language that we can understand. She is presented as a martyr among persons in the medical community, while the others are presented as only out for power, money, and fame. In her first conversation with Ned she asks if he has had any of the symptoms of the illness. Ned replies that he has had "most of the sexually transmitted diseases the article [in the *New York Times*] said come first."[16] The conversation continues:

> EMMA: . . . Any fever, weight loss, night sweats, diarrhea, swollen glands, white patches in your mouth, loss of energy, shortness of breath, chronic cough?
>
> NED: No. But those could happen with a lot of things, couldn't they?
>
> EMMA: And purple lesions. Sometimes. Which is what I'm looking for. It's a cancer. There seems to be a strange action in the immune system. It's collapsed. Won't work. Won't fight. Which is what it's supposed to do. So most of the diseases my guys are coming down with—and there are some very strange ones—are caused by germs that wouldn't hurt a baby, not a baby in New York City anyway. Unfortunately, the immune system is the system we know least about.[17]

While this information provides a relatively straightforward account of what AIDS is, most of the play tells us that it is only affecting gay men. In this play, AIDS is a "gay disease" transmitted through sexual contact. Only once is heterosexual transmission explicitly referred to in the play. This reference occurs during Dr. Brookner's argument with the doctor who denies her funding for research. She states, "Women have been discovered to have it in Africa—where it is clearly transmitted heterosexually. It is only a question of time. We could all be dead before you do anything."[18]

Finally, perhaps the best information about AIDS is the collection of facts, statistics, dates, and names that are painted on the set and the walls of the performance space—a theatrical strategy similar to the Brechtian technique of signposting.[19] Kramer explains that in the production at the Public Theater, "Everywhere possible, on this set and upon the theater walls too, facts and figures and names were painted in black, simple lettering."[20] One item included in this production was the number of persons with AIDS throughout the United States. These figures, obtained from the Center for Disease Control, were continuously updated, crossing out the old number and replacing it with the new. The set also included the names of persons who died. There were also a number of items on the set that implicated various institutions for their inactivity in the AIDS crisis. A comparison was drawn between the amount of money Mayor Feinstein (of San Francisco) and Mayor Koch (of New York) allotted for AIDS education and services. Other comparisons were drawn between the amount of press coverage AIDS received in different newspapers.[21]

Each of these elements appears to function as a means of connecting the fictional, theatrical world to the real world. As Ann Fettner explains:

> When Joel Grey [the actor who played Ned Weeks] shouted something about there already being 40 deaths in New York City alone, all eyes cut to the number "4280" hanging over the center stage. And shuddered.[22]

Productions using this technique remind the audience of the impact that AIDS has had throughout the world. Also, the inclusion of items, such as the number of articles written on the virus in comparison to other epidemics, further indicts institutions for their lethargy during the early stages of the AIDS crisis.[23] It could be argued that while the play itself implies that AIDS is a "gay disease," these scenic elements resignify AIDS to include more than just gay men. However, it is unlikely that the small number of scenic elements that attempt to resignify AIDS (as opposed to those attempting to implicate various institutions) have such a strong impact on the audience. Finally, performances that do not use this technique may fail to make the connections between the real and fictional worlds, explicit enough for the audience to read it as a "true story" rather than a purely fictional account.

Because *The Normal Heart* is based on actual events that occurred between the years 1981 and 1984, the play can be viewed as a docudrama about the early years in the AIDS crisis. Although the names have been changed, Kramer's play is rooted largely in his own experiences with the Gay Men's Health Crisis. As Holleran explains in his introduction to the play:

> *The Normal Heart* is, after all, a history play—of the past five years: a period in which thousands died. There is really nothing more to say to introduce a play in which you will find virtually every fact, statistic, issue, anguish, lament, and question alluded to here. Neither is there any way to discuss this play as drama. . . . It is a hunk of reality that has been depicted for us, so current that, to paraphrase a film critic, the sirens you hear on stage are the sirens you hear when you walk out of the theater.[24]

Holleran implies that the choice to base the play on actual events affords it more credibility than *As Is*. By incorporating raw factual data into the scenic elements and by building the plot from historical events, Kramer's play may appear more realistic and perhaps more persuasive than plays that are fictional. The assumption seems to be that if people cannot leave the theater and say "it was just a play," then they may be more apt to do something about the AIDS crisis.

Perhaps as an attempt to make the play even more realistic, Kramer also incorporated fragments from articles he wrote during the early stages of the crisis. When the organization meets to mail out flyers, Mickey reads what Ned had written for the flyer, but which he refused to include because he believed it was too harsh:

> MICKEY: . . . This is what Ned wrote for me to send out. "If this doesn't scare the shit out of you, and rouse you to action, gay men have no future on earth."
>
> BRUCE: You're crazy.

NED: Shake up. What's wrong with that? This isn't something that can be force-fed gently; it won't work. Mickey neglected to read my first sentence.

MICKEY: "It's difficult to write this without sounding alarmist or scared." Okay, but then listen to this: "I am sick of guys moaning that giving up careless sex until this blows over is worse than death . . . I am sick of guys who can only think with their cocks . . . I am sick of closeted gays. It's 1982 now, guys, when are you going to come out? By 1984 you could be dead."[25]

The argument continues and Ned finally says that he is going to get the *Native* (a gay newspaper in New York) to run the article. The article did, in fact, appear in the *New York Native* in March of 1983 and, Kramer explains, "was reprinted in almost every major gay newspaper across the country."[26]

Another point of comparison between these two plays involves the fact that both are "gay plays" in that they deal with gay characters and subject matter (or at least the issue is presented as such), and are written by openly gay authors. Additionally, according to John Clum, both plays could be characterized as "domestic dramas." According to Clum, there exist three impulses exist in gay drama as a whole: (1) the historical, (2) the anarchic, and (3) the domestic. The history drama is a play that depicts the "oppression and resistance and survival and heroic making" of male homosexuals in order to achieve a sense of commonality within the gay, male community.[27] Additionally, Clum argues, the historical impulse is also a means of educating the dominant (i.e., heterosexual) culture about the effects of its homophobia.[28]

The second impulse, the anarchic impulse, is found in plays that make fun of the dominant culture "in favor of creative chaos which allows free expression of sexual impulses."[29] Clum cites Joe Orton's plays as exemplifying the anarchic impulse. Orton, a British playwright whose works include *Entertaining Mr. Sloane* (1964) and *Loot* (1966), wrote comic plays condemning social institutions and enjoyed "shocking people."[30]

Domestic dramas call "for assimilation through domestication. . . . In gay domestic drama . . . the celebration of a gay marriage or 'family' establishes and affirms commonality with the 'straight' audience."[31] Domestic dramas appear to be the ones most receptive to "straight" audiences. Thus, as Clive Barnes suggests, "Both plays are written by homosexuals, about homosexuals, but not, specifically, for homosexuals. They deal with death and suffering—the tragic commonplaces of human experience."[32] This attempt to universalize the messages of both plays, moving them out of "gay" life and attempting to make them appropriate for straight audiences, is a theme found in many of the reviews of these plays.

As Is and *The Normal Heart*, Clum argues, could be called domestic dramas, although each utilizes a different strategy of achieving "commonality" with a heterosexual audience. In *The Normal Heart*, Ned's argument for gay men to stop having sex is coupled with his belief that they need to be in monogamous relationships. Monogamy is one of the two primary themes or messages of the play and is reflected in Ned's relationship with Felix.[33] In one of his many arguments with Bruce and other members of the organization, Ned shows how he is attempting to get these men to realize that gay culture should not be defined solely in terms of its sexual practices:

> BRUCE: But we can't tell people how to live their lives! We can't do that. And besides, the entire gay political platform is fucking. We'd get it from all sides.
>
> NED: You make it sound like that's all that being gay means.
>
> BRUCE: That's all it does mean!
>
> MICKEY: It's the only thing that makes us different.
>
> NED: I don't want to be considered different. . . . Why is it we can only talk about our sexuality, and so relentlessly? You know, Mickey, all we've created is generations of guys who can't deal with each other as anything but erections.[34]

By arguing against sex as the sole means of gay identity, Ned may become a more sympathetic character to a mainstream, heterosexual audience. In addition, Ned confesses that although he has been promiscuous in the past, he does not approve of it or "like [himself] for doing it."[35] Confessing his past "sins" may prompt heterosexual audiences to become more sympathetic to his cause. And, because Ned is arguing for relationships modelled after heterosexual relationships, he seems to solicit sympathy from the heterosexuals who see the play. As John Clum explains, the relationship between Ned and Felix "affirms gay marriage as the model for relationships and as a counter to deadly promiscuity."[36] Seymour Kleinberg presents a more ironic attitude toward this theme when he argues, "The love that the play advocates is not only romantic and monogamous, it is conventional married love, blessed by higher authorities."[37]

Additionally, *The Normal Heart* attempts to achieve this commonality by drawing links between the Holocaust and AIDS. On his first date with Felix, Ned explains:

> Do you know that when Hitler's Final Solution to eliminate Polish Jews was first mentioned in the *Times* it was on page twenty-eight. And on page six of the *Washington Post*. And the *Times* and the *Post* were owned by Jews. What causes silence like that? Why didn't the American Jews help the German Jews get out? Their very own people! Scholars are finally writing honestly about this—I've been doing some research—and it's damning to everyone who was here then: Jewish leadership for being totally ineffective; Jewish organizations for constantly fighting among themselves, unable to cooperate even in the face of death.[38]

Because everyone knows about the Holocaust, Kramer's analogy becomes another means through which the mainstream theater audience can come to understand the AIDS issue. This analogy, however, is not without problems, according to some. Sy Syna, for example, finds it "an ethnic affront" because, she argues, homosexuals have brought AIDS on themselves. She further argues that homosexuals have a means to prevent the spread of AIDS, which the play argues for. She concludes her argument by stating that such an analogy "is offensive to anyone except a homosexual who feels that society has an obligation to pick up the tab for the unsavory implications of their lifestyle."[39]

As Is presents the love and commitment between two gay men. As I stated earlier, Hoffman has argued that he did not write a play about AIDS, but about a relationship between two men. Like *The*

Normal Heart, As Is downplays the role of sex and focuses on a monogamous relationship in order to make the play more acceptable for mainstream audiences. Hoffman claims that his play is for everybody and that he "had to diffuse the issue of sex for straight and gay audiences alike, so that we could get beyond it."[40]

It should be noted, however, that Hoffman's play does not take the same stance toward the sexual practices of the gay community as Kramer's. Monogamy is not explicitly advocated in *As Is*; it is simply the relationship that we see most often in the play. While the main characters, especially Rich, seem to lament the loss of casual sex, none of the men openly condemns the gay community for the spread of AIDS. As Richard Goldstein remarks, "Hoffman demands that gay men and their institutions be embraced intact—as is."[41]

Not only are the relationships in these plays modelled after those considered most acceptable, but so too are the occupations of the major characters. As Gevisser explains, both plays "take place within the urban bourgeois culture of successful gay arts-professionals" (50). Hence, the occupations of the major characters become another means through which mainstream audiences come to accept and approve of the plays.

In *The Normal Heart*, Felix and Ned are both writers; in *As Is*, Saul is a photographer and Rich a writer. Also, few of the characters are members of the working class, all appear to be white, and few of the characters are female. In fact, neither play spends a significant amount of time talking about any community that has been affected by the epidemic except for male homosexuals.

In *As Is*, a few references are made to people outside of the white, male homosexual community. First, early in the play the television announcer, in a prerecorded speech, tells us that "the disease is beginning to make inroads into the general population";[42] however, his speech overlaps with a conversation between Rich and his doctors. As a result, the announcer's comment may be missed. A second example occurs in the scene where the chorus members talk about the first memorial service they attended.[43] This segment concludes with a list of approximately thirty names, only two of which are female (Julie and Marie), and a few other male names that could be read as stereotypical representatives of a minority group (e.g., Jamal).

In *The Normal Heart*, Mickey mentions the importance of getting others involved in the organization, although no mention is made of the impact of the virus on these groups; they seem to want members of these other marginalized groups to help them with their cause, without admitting the impact that the virus could have or has had on these communities.[44] Mickey admits, "I'm worried this organization might only attract white bread and middle-class. We need blacks." The conversation continues, revealing to the audience the dichotomy that exists within the gay community between lesbians and gay men:

> MICKEY: . . . and . . . how do you feel about Lesbians?
>
> BRUCE: Not very much. I mean, they're . . . something else.
>
> MICKEY: I wonder what they're going to think about all this? If past history is any guide, there's never been much support by either half of us for the other.[45]

A few lines before this interaction we also are made aware of the conflict within the gay, male community between the "transvestites" and the "Brooks Brothers" types:

> MICKEY: You know, the battle against the police at Stonewall was won by transvestites. We all fought like hell. It's you Brooks Brothers guys who—
>
> BRUCE: That's why I wasn't at Stonewall. I don't have anything in common with those guys, girls, whatever you call them.[46]

Both of these exchanges reveal issues that surfaced long before the AIDS crisis; it is only within the crisis that they become more apparent. Some gay men (as Bruce's comments suggest) attempt to deny the fact that other groups are affected by AIDS and imply that some gay men are superior to others. Such a belief is quite ironic in that the groups Bruce mentions (lesbians and transvestites) are, like all gay men, marginalized members of society.

Finally, both these plays incorporate defamiliarization techniques we have come to associate with Brecht. In *As Is*, there is a chorus, and not only do the members of the chorus remain on stage throughout the performance, they play all the minor roles in the play. As Mel Gussow argues:

> To a certain degree, Mr. Hoffman is practicing theatrical alienation. By having all the actors and actresses, except for Mr. Hogan and Mr. Hadary [Rich and Saul], play a cross section of characters and remain on stage as overseeing and often interacting chorus, he is expanding the boundaries of naturalism. He is also restoring the audience's moment-to-moment identification.[47]

Gussow further argues that because Rich's brother plays a variety of other roles throughout the play, his scene with Rich is not as "tearful" (3). In addition, the chorus sometimes addresses the audience, breaking down the "fourth wall" and differentiating the play from more realistic types of drama. Similarly, in *The Normal Heart*, Kramer's minimal settings are used as a method that allows the play to distance itself from more naturalist, realist plays. As Kramer explains, the Public Theater's production "was conceived as exceptionally simple."[48]

The use of such techniques differentiates the plays from traditional, classic realist dramas. But it is unlikely that such techniques will be regarded by contemporary audiences as novel or meaningful, much less political, revolutionary, or avant-garde. As Elizabeth Wright argues (admitting that others have made this point), Brechtian theater has been divorced from its political origins, and his techniques have become "the universal language for contemporary theatre." In fact, she says, "The techniques of montage, of epic narration, of diverse visual and auditory effects are used far more radically [in contemporary theatre, film, and television] than they are in Brecht's own plays."[49]

In summary, through a comparison of the texts of these plays, their success in mainstream theater is easy to explain. AIDS and gay culture are distanced from the mainstream audience; AIDS is signified primarily as a "gay disease," since only gay men in these plays have AIDS.[50] Finally, the main characters in each of these plays are young, white, middle-class professionals—yuppies. Those attending these plays can associate with the characters as middle-class professionals, but still maintain a safe distance from them as gay men and as persons with AIDS. As a result, these plays themselves become acceptable or "safe" for mainstream theater audiences.

Before discussing the critical responses to these plays, I want to note some additional differences between these plays outside of the texts themselves. Although both plays can be viewed as mainstream, conventional theater, only *As Is* made it to Broadway—the prototype of American, mainstream theater. Like the most famous and successful gay plays that made it to Broadway (e.g., *La Cage Aux Folles* and *Torch Song Trilogy*), *As Is* presents a gay relationship that is modelled after the traditional, heterosexual relationship. Would a play that dealt with IV drug users, unwed mothers, prostitutes, or others who could be viewed as more marginalized than middle-class, professional male homosexuals appear in a mainstream theater? It seems highly unlikely that such plays would obtain the same level of success achieved by *As Is* and *The Normal Heart*. Domesticating these gay relationships makes them safe for mainstream theater audiences.

While *The Normal Heart* advocates such relationships, the amount of time spent showing this relationship is quite minimal when compared to *As Is*. Also, *The Normal Heart*'s overt criticism of the government and medical establishment differentiates it from the non-argumentative, humanistic approach to AIDS that we find in *As Is*. Similarly, while gay plays that make it to Broadway commonly evoke sympathy for gay persons, they rarely raise the audience's consciousness regarding gay rights.[51] As Gevisser argues:

> William Hoffman's *As Is* . . . is a beautifully wrought AIDS drama that played successfully on Broadway for months and was adapted for public television. Humanizing people with AIDS, it is, like *Torch Song*, a tearjerker that elicits much sympathy from its audience. But tears shed from sympathy dry up by the time you've crossed the lobby to the busy street outside and you're deciding where to eat.
>
> If you were to shed any tears at all in Larry Kramer's *The Normal Heart*, on the other hand, they would be tears of rage. . . . With jeremiad prophesies and loose (often irresponsible)

> analogies made between the AIDS epidemic and the Holocaust, *The
> Normal Heart* is calculated to enrage and inflame its audience: its
> express intention has been to mobilize people into action once they
> leave the theater. It never made it to Broadway.[52]

Gevisser implies that only those gay plays that "humanize" gay people
(and persons with AIDS) and/or perpetuate stereotypes will be
successful, i.e., make it to Broadway.

A final difference between these two plays is that *As Is* was
presented in another medium. Like *Torch Song Trilogy* and *La Cage
Aux Folles*, which were made into movies, *As Is* was presented on
Showtime, directed by Michael Lindsay-Hogg (the director of the Public
Theater production of *The Normal Heart*). Kramer's attempt to get *The
Normal Heart* made into a movie is still pending. He has negotiated a
deal with Barbra Streisand, who is supposed to produce, direct, and play
the role of Dr. Brookner. In *Reports from the Holocaust*, Kramer
explains that because Streisand decided to direct *Nuts* first, a movie he
thought was terrible, he decided he did not want her to film *The Normal
Heart*.[53] However, it seems that Kramer has changed his mind. In a
recent column in *POV*, Bruce Bibby quotes Barbra Streisand as saying,
"His play, *The Normal Heart*, is a universal story about everyone's right
to love. I'm proud that he has entrusted it to us to bring to the screen."[54]
Her comment implies that as of early 1995, she still intends to make a
movie version of the play. But since it has yet to make it to the screen,
and never made it to Broadway or television, it could be argued that *As
Is* was more successful than *The Normal Heart*.

CRITICAL RESPONSES

In 1989, Larry Kramer's second play dealing with the AIDS
issue, *Just Say No: A Play About a Farce*, was published.[55] In his
introduction to the play, Kramer presents his version of American
theater and its critics:

> It seems to me that the more a play is *about* something—an opinion,
> a philosophy, a specific point of view—the more the critic feels

> bound to attack it. The modern play, to be "artistically correct,"
> must not take sides, ruffle feathers, churn up waters, make you
> think. . . . It definitely must not be critical of the status quo—i.e.,
> the trendies themselves; we are not a nation good at either
> criticizing or laughing at ourselves.[56]

He later continues:

> American theater reflects an inordinate inability to laugh
> at ourselves, to criticize the powers-that-be. How exceptionally
> boring. And polite. . . .
> When something comes along that is offensive, and is
> meant to be offensive—actually aggressively affronting current
> thinking, actually struggling with determination to crash through a
> brick wall of apathy or denial or ignorance--today's theater of
> boring politesse is now so entrenched, and the critics now say "You
> must write more coldly" so automatically, that what should be the
> true nature of the playwright's calling is not only overlooked, *it* is
> found to be offensive.[57]

Kramer's statements are congruent with many of the responses to *The
Normal Heart* and *Just Say No*, both of which level fierce attacks
against "the powers-that-be." Kramer believes that it was his
condemnation of Ronald Reagan in *Just Say No* that led to its lack of
success. Because reviewers believed he had gone too far, they closed his
show.[58]

Certainly, critics do have some power in regards to the success
or failure of a given performance. For a significant part of the
mainstream theater audience, critiques of various plays do determine
whether or not people will see them. In addition, these reviews often
predetermine the responses of audience members. Because critics cannot
possibly discuss all elements of a given performance, they choose to
emphasize some elements and ignore or pay less attention to others. As
a result, critics can affect how audience members "read" a play.

Because *As Is* and *The Normal Heart* are contemporaries, a
number of the reviewers have drawn comparisons between them. And
when these comparisons are drawn, it is usually *As Is* that wins the
"best AIDS play" award. Even in the reviews that deal with the plays

individually, the pattern that seems to emerge is that *As Is* is a better play, a better *gay* play, and a better *AIDS* play.

It could be argued that, especially in a capitalistic society, a good play or drama is one that is popular, that is, one that achieves commercial success. According to such standards, both *As Is* and *The Normal Heart* are good plays. However, such criteria do little to explain what makes a play successful. Critics have additional standards through which they make their evaluations of a given text and, for the purposes of this study, it is important to understand their criteria. The reviews of these plays indicate that many critics judged these plays in terms of traditional or modernist views of drama.

One of the themes found in critical responses to these shows is universality. And when these plays are praised for their universality, they are also made safe for the heterosexual audience by implying that these plays are tragedies to which *all* people can relate. The "universal message makes a good play" criterion is found in reviews published in both *Time* and *Newsweek*. In *Time*, William Henry states, "What makes *As Is* and *The Normal Heart* so deeply affecting is that they portray anguish and doom in individual human terms and enable audiences of every sexual inclination to grasp a common bond of suffering and mortality."[59] *Newsweek*'s Jack Kroll has a similar response to these plays: "These plays . . . are not 'homosexual' plays; they enact situations and raise questions of universal concern for everyone, straight or gay, male or female."[60] Rob Baker, speaking solely about *As Is,* also uses traditional dramatic standards to judge the play when he states that the play "holds up remarkably well in the mid-nineties as a work of character, drama, and ideas—peppered throughout with humor, information, and humanity."[61]

Hence, for some critics these plays are neither "gay plays" nor "AIDS plays" because they transcend the issue of AIDS and homosexuality, turning AIDS into a metaphor for individual suffering—something that everyone can understand because they are human beings. The audience identifies and empathizes with these characters and with their situations, even though they are gay. Finally, the audience members are purged of these emotions; that is, by the end of the play, they are relieved because they have experienced a certain kind of emotional sharing. Clive Barnes' review of *As Is* seems to argue for a cleansing function of dramatic texts, as well as for plays that address "universal" issues. He states, "I doubt whether *As Is* will prove unduly popular with the homosexual community—its problems must be too near home."[62] Such remarks suggest that when an issue is too topical, too "near to home," we cannot possibly be purged; that is, that drama is supposed to deal with issues that are not too close to us, for if they are, emotional cleansing cannot take place. On the other hand, Shewey argues:

> The line between what was happening on stage and what was happening in the lives of the audience was so fine that the script for these works [which include *As Is* and *The Normal Heart*] seemed a mere pretext for the gathering of individuals collectively seeking information about this mysterious disease, seeking an outlet for anger, anxiety, and grief. These plays had a powerful impact on an audience that needed to bolster a still shaky sense of gay self-acceptance in order to face the medical horrors and political backlash sure to come.[63]

Hence, Shewey suggests that these plays provide an emotional outlet for homosexuals: they are an "outlet" for expressing grief, anger, etc.

Some critics describe these plays as *political* dramas rather than universal dramas, because both, in some ways, appear to challenge the status quo. Indeed, critics often praise them as such and draw parallels between them and Brecht's work. However, the comparison to Brecht is not without its difficulties. In her review of *The Normal Heart*, Fettner explains how Kramer experienced the same problems as other didactic or political playwrights:

> Didactic theater is hard to take. It goes against thousands of years of Western theatrical tradition, in which the actors' masks inform the audience what they need to feel, so that catharsis can take place. . . . Audiences are not accustomed to, nor do they desire to go to the theater to *think*. Even those modern plays designated "thoughtful" rarely concern immediate societal issues.[64]

Although Kramer's play is certainly one of these "thoughtful" plays, Fettner suggests that he fell into the same trap as Brecht did with *Mother Courage*. That is, the audience's need to identify with a character or characters prevents it from responding critically to the political issues:

> Like Mother Courage, the Kramer character loses virtually everything. But, also like Courage, he bundles up his wares and struggles on again after the retreating army. It is the struggle with which the audience identifies and sighs with relief; finally the cathartic moment: we can leave the theater emptied. In the wings, of course, the playwright bangs his head against the wall: it hasn't worked again![65]

Thus, Fettner argues that *The Normal Heart* seems to fail in the same way that most political plays addressing a mainstream audience fail. Audiences are so conditioned to "read" plays empathetically, they can transform even the fiercest attack on their values into pleasurable, emotionally cleansing entertainments.

Hence, when these plays are viewed as mainstream drama, the criteria through which they are judged may serve to help us appreciate them as works of art, but such an appreciation may supplant political understanding. The critics suggest that these plays are good because they teach us about human suffering, not about AIDS or homosexuality. Indeed, the plays are good precisely because they transcend the local and particular to address universal themes. Additionally, because traditional theater audiences want to identify with or feel compassion toward the characters, they can come away feeling cleansed rather than "politicized" by the theater experience.

When these plays are read as "gay plays," a different set of issues comes to the forefront. Broadly stated, these issues concern whether—and how—gay people should be represented on stage. First, as Patrick Merla explains, attempts to censor these two plays stem from the belief that representing homosexuality is a type of proselytizing for homosexuality. For example, PBS refused to air *As Is* for fear that it would be accused of "promulgating homosexuality."[66] The play did air on Showtime with some revisions, such as changing some of the four-letter words. In fact, the graphic language was another objection raised to both plays. Feingold responds to such attempts at censorship by stating:

> the morally relativistic absurdity of complaining about dirty words while babies wither away and die from opportunistic infections does not seem to have occurred to these well meaning souls, who would rather protect their ears than their grandchildren.[67]

The fact that both these plays do not, except in passing, discuss any other group affected by AIDS outside of male homosexuals, does not seem to be relevant to Feingold. Perhaps if these plays did attempt to challenge the idea that AIDS was a "gay disease," attempts to censor the plays for both reasons might not exist.

A more significant issue, perhaps, especially in the case of *The Normal Heart*, is how gay persons are represented. And this issue has sparked a great deal of controversy. Richard Goldstein explains heterosexual and homosexual responses to these plays. He begins by asking why Kramer has received more publicity than Hoffman. His answer to the question is that the responses to *The Normal Heart* were largely divided, with heterosexual critics praising the play and gay critics condemning it. This dichotomy, he argues:

> says a lot about the way liberal heterosexuals view gay rights in general and gay life in particular. They're committed to the former and ambivalent about the latter, and Larry Kramer gives them ammunition for both positions. Hoffman demands that gay men and their institutions be embraced intact—as is. But Kramer tells straight people it is okay to support gay rights while condemning the way we live.[68]

Goldstein provides one explanation for the differing responses of gay and straight critics.

One specific criticism by gay critics of both plays, but mostly of *The Normal Heart*, is that neither addresses the real issues. Kleinberg describes this problem as one of "gay identity"; that is, what does being a homosexual mean? He states, "As long as the subject of gay identity is argued in terms of whether it is good or bad, legitimate or illegitimate, there is no energy left to address the question of what it is."[69] Clum raises a similar question in his response to *The Normal Heart*. He states, "Kramer posits resistance as the only stance to the indifference or oppression of the dominant culture. . . . Yet what is lost in the process of this resistance is a celebration of what that non-sexual culture is."[70] Kleinberg also raises a question related specifically to *The Normal Heart* and, in doing so, seems to lament the fact that the play is attempting to be universal and, thus, ignores the more specific issue of what it is like to be a gay man in America. According to Kleinberg, "The play doesn't ask: why am I dying of AIDS? But it does ask: why have I been chosen by that same random Nature to suffer outsidedness when, like every man in America, I was told I was born to privilege?"[71]

Kleinberg and Clum argue that a large part of gay identity involves a certain style of humor. And although neither Kleinberg nor Clum uses the term, what they seem to be implying is that *The Normal Heart* lacks "camp"—the form of ironic humor that is usually associated with gay men.[72] Both writers condemn Kramer's exclusion of this "gay wit." Kleinberg asserts, "It is a bit ironic that gay men as a group are noted for their acerbic wit, their radical and impeccable taste, their critical sensibility, yet the plays have succeeded because they are sentimental and full of bathos."[73] Similarly, in regard to *The Normal Heart*, Clum points out:

> Except for some wit from Ned's lover, Felix, there is no sense of play, of theatricality, of the wit that protects and assaults. . . .
>
> The gay experience has always been highly theatrical, and gay history needs to celebrate the theatricality even in celebrating the martyrdom, the sense of play as the alternative to oppression.[74]

Thus, for some gay critics, these plays do not help gay persons deal with what it means to be gay. More specifically, these plays do not help homosexuals redefine themselves, as the plays argue they should, outside of their sexual practices. They are, for some critics, gay plays (because they include predominantly gay characters) that do not deal adequately with gay issues.

Finally, while all critiques of these plays mention the AIDS issue, a number of critics suggest that the plays should be judged as "AIDS plays," a category that in effect exempts them from the norms and standards of dramatic art. Perhaps the best example of such criticism appears in Gerald Weales' "AIDS on Stage: Advocacy and Ovations." In a review of both plays, Weales argues:

> Neither work seems to me particularly distinguished as a play, but the enthusiastic and obviously moved audiences are not simply expressing their approval of the plays and the performances, which are fine in both cases. They are responding to the subject matter, showing their sympathy for the courage of AIDS victims offstage as well as on, and—particularly in *The Normal Heart*—their anger that more has not been done to discover the causes and stem the growth of so frightening a disease. Nor are these simply gay audiences responding to an epidemic that has hit the gay community the hardest. The audiences are mixed; the response is not.[75]

Similarly, Kleinberg writes, "The modest commercial success but large artistic failures of the plays about AIDS says something about the response of audiences to the crisis." Hence, what both Weales and Kleinberg are implying is that these are not good plays in the traditional sense of the word, but they are appealing because they deal with an issue that mainstream audiences find important or timely.

The comments by Weales and Kleinberg could be read as a veiled critique of the audiences, the playwrights, or perhaps both. Such reviews suggest, on the one hand, that the audiences of these plays lack discrimination. Unlike the critics, audiences are unable to distinguish "good drama" from topical drama. On the other hand, these statements imply that both Hoffman and Kramer are merely pandering to the public, lowering their standards in order to produce something that is popular. Regardless of how their comments are read, the category "AIDS plays" enables critics like Weales and Kleinberg to account for the popularity of such plays while still holding on to their aesthetic standards.

A more controversial response to these plays is presented by Michael Feingold in his introduction to his collection of plays about

AIDS entitled *The Way We Live Now*. In this text, Feingold exhibits what Gevisser calls a "nakedly elitist valorization of lives" that is "terrifying."[76] Feingold argues:

> [W]e are urged, subtly, to view each death [from AIDS] as the equivalent of each other. . . . [B]ut . . . it is deeply and outrageously untrue, . . . because many of those affected are artists in their creative prime, and what an artist gives to the world is not the same as ordinary souls doing their jobs and leading their ordinary lives. I am sorry for the brute fact, but when an accountant dies, there is another accountant; when Mozart dies, there may be Beethoven, but that is something quite different.[77]

This appalling comment, Gevisser argues, fails to recognize that because *all* homosexuals are "a stigmatized and disenfranchised minority," they "acquire political power by mourning collectively as well as individually."[78] Gevisser continues:

> [I]f an accountant is dispensable, how low on his chart of worth would he rate a baby with AIDS, a welfare mother with AIDS, a drug addict with AIDS? Is he suggesting that the epidemic is only a tragedy insofar as it robs our culture of its creative gay men? For if he is, he is dispensing with most of the people who are sick in much the same way that gay people have been dispensed with since the beginning of this epidemic.
>
> His approach underscores the general direction theater about AIDS has taken: it veers more toward humanist tragedy—the expression and working through of individual grief—than toward the defining of a collective political and social identity around a common experience of oppression and marginalization. The AIDS crisis is perceived not as a national disaster, but as something that has challenged the little niche professional and creative gay men have carved for themselves within urban bourgeois society.[79]

Hence, both these plays ignore other classes in favor of the one class, as Feingold argues, that gives so much to the dominant culture. But such an approach to the epidemic, as Gevisser argues (and I would certainly agree), is not very different from the responses of the dominant culture to the epidemic. Because male homosexuals are not considered part of the "general population" and AIDS is viewed as a gay disease, little attention was paid, especially early on, to the virus.

Gevisser argues that "theater about AIDS" tends to veer "more toward humanistic tragedy—the expression and working through of individual grief—than toward the defining of a collective political and social identity around a common experience of oppression and marginalization."[80] And it is precisely the humanistic and rather individualistic approach that each of these plays takes toward the issue of AIDS that makes them, like AIDS itself, safe for a "general population." If these plays did not attempt to establish some common ground between the gay community and the "general population," it is highly unlikely that either would have been as successful, commercially or critically. But whether that "success" should be interpreted as an indication of "failure" at the political level, as critics like Feingold, Fettner, and Gevisser suggest, is still a matter of controversy.

EFFECTIVENESS

To conclude this chapter I want to discuss the efficacy of these performances for social change. Although I have argued that both plays attempt (in various ways) to make themselves safe for mainstream theater audiences, this does not necessarily mean that these plays cannot promote the kind of political knowledge or action that might lead to social change.

In his essay "The Transparent Closet: Gay Theater for Straight Audiences," Richard Hall suggests, "Theater is inefficient as an instrument for social change. It either speaks to those already in support of its views, or to those who are so secure in their power that they don't mind hearing themselves abused, as long as the abuse is entertaining."[81] He continues, "Gay life, if it is to transfer to the Majestic or the Booth, must be prettified and detoxified."[82] Similarly, Gevisser argues that there are certain "costumes and poses gay people adopt to play at the Straight-Boy Cafe."[83] He later states:

> [R]ealpolitik . . . is anathema to the system of Broadway, which
> has beat a retreat fast and furious through the eighties into the
> world of escapism and pure fantasy: men in feather boas are as

otherworldly as a bunch of funny-named Cats in an oversized junkyard or a Phantom who inhabits an old opera house. If *Torch Song* challenged or confronted its audience, it would close in a week, just as Emily Mann's *Execution of Justice* did in 1986.[84]

Both Gevisser and Hall seem to suggest that in order for plays to make it to Broadway, they must make some compromises in terms of their politics. Additionally, both argue, for different reasons, that theater is not an effective tool for social change.

However, *The Normal Heart* did spark a great deal of controversy. As Feingold argues, the aggressiveness through which the play addresses AIDS led to censorship battles. Such controversies, he suggests, "have revealed—as if we didn't already know—that the American public, in 1990 remains as confused and uninformed about the nature of art as about that of AIDS."[85] Nowhere was this controversy more apparent than in Springfield, Missouri.

In November of 1989, the theater department at Southwest Missouri State University staged a production of *The Normal Heart* that received national attention.[86] Approximately two weeks prior to the production, a full page advertisement appeared in the Sunday edition of the *Springfield News-Leader* denouncing the production. Paid for by a group calling itself "Citizens Demanding Standards," the ad argued that the play should be cancelled. According to the advertisement, *The Normal Heart* is a "homosexual play" that "was written by a militant homosexual political activist."[87] They argue that the play:

A.   PROMOTES HOMOSEXUAL LIFE-STYLE AS NORMAL
B.   ADVOCATES A MILITANT HOMOSEXUAL POLITICAL AGENDA
C.   DEMONSTRATES IGNORANCE AS TO CAUSE AND PREVENTION OF A DEADLY VIRUS
D.   USES UNNECESSARY PROFANITY

The ad continues, presenting "facts" about homosexuality and AIDS, and asks readers to write their representatives to let them know they object to the play and the use of their tax dollars to "promote homosexual, anti-family life-style."[88]

After the advertisement appeared, letters and phone calls began to arrive at the theater office in support and protest of the production. Letters and articles about the controversy were also published in the local newspaper. Television news crews made requests to attend rehearsals. Famous alumni, including Tess Harper, John Goodman, and Kathleen Turner, became involved and, as a result, the national media began to cover the controversy. When tickets went on sale, all the performances were sold out in three-and-a-half hours.

Two days before the production was to open, protesters of the performance held a rally. The next day, State Representative Jean Dixon, along with various media persons, went to the president of the university and demanded to be seen. While there, Dixon delivered a petition with 5,000 signatures that demanded cancelling the show. At the same time, a rally in support of the production was held. Organized by a group called PACT, People Acting with Compassion and Tolerance, the rally included Tess Harper and others who spoke about gay and AIDS issues.

When opening night came, the building was checked for bombs, and a metal detector was installed at the entrance to check for weapons. Prior to the performance, a candlelight vigil was held in support of the production. Outside the theater, one protestor was found handing out pamphlets that denounced homosexuality. Inside, the theater lobby was filled with security people, state news media personnel, and a crew from CNN.

While the president of PACT, Brad Evans, was attending the vigil, his house was set on fire. The fire destroyed the house and killed his two cats.[89] As a result of the fire, the president of the university decided that the cast and others involved with the performance should be put in a motel for the night. The police were asked to check the homes of these people.

When Dixon was asked about the fire, she said that the fire was probably set by Evans himself, whom she described as a known Satan worshipper and that he had probably sacrificed his cats as part of a ritual. Later, Dixon denied that she had made these statements, insisting that she had been "misquoted." The rest of the performances went on as scheduled and without incident.

Howard Averback suggests that because of the controversy surrounding the production, a number of positive changes took place in the community.[90] First, the publicity resulted in a large number of people seeing the production. Second, AIDS awareness increased and the desire to learn more about AIDS was higher than it had been in the past. In fact, Bradley notes that the desire for information about AIDS was so high, that in the four weeks prior to the production, the health clinic gave out more information on AIDS than they had given out the entire year.[91] Third, the administration at the university, through its support of the production, reaffirmed its belief in freedom of expression. Finally, the controversy led to an increase in activism from people who were once apolitical.

Most importantly, however, the community became a space for public debates about homosexuality and AIDS. Because the controversy became such a public issue, it forced people to take sides, to debate issues that had been ignored or silenced within this community. It should be noted that most of these debates centered on the legitimacy of homosexuality, rather than the politics of AIDS. As Averback explains, the purpose of the production was AIDS education, but this issue "took a back seat" to other ethical issues.[92]

The controversy that occurred in Springfield suggests that theater can promote social change. But such changes may only occur when a play's "meaning" or "message" is taken out of its immediate context and brought into other public spaces. In other words, the link between theater and social change is not a direct, cause/effect relationship. Performances dealing with AIDS, or with gay issues occurring within the confines of the mainstream theaters are usually "preaching to the converted," as Hall suggests, i.e., those in support of the viewpoint advocated by the play. Performances may provide sympathy for these people; however, unless some controversy is raised outside the theater, it is unlikely that any significant changes will occur.

In his introduction to *Just Say No*, Larry Kramer also responds to the question of whether or not theater can promote social change. He states:

> Did *The Normal Heart* change the world? Of course not. But it did accomplish more than a little something here and there. It has been produced all over America and all over the world, including such unlikely places as South Africa, Russia, and Poland (and Poland is a land where there is such homophobia that gay people often commit suicide). In Lafayette, Louisiana, a town where they beat up gay people in the streets, the play was done by an amateur group, in a run that was extended twice and then repeated a year later; local straights joined the few local gays who were out of the closet to form an AIDS service organization. And, in Baton Rouge, the local drama critic came out of the closet in his review.

Kramer also argues that although his play condemned the *New York Times*, its "AIDS coverage is now better than it ever was." Finally, he argues that his play offered a "dramatic argument" which "has entered the general discourse on the history of AIDS"—that the AIDS crisis was allowed to grow because Mayor Koch "is a closeted homosexual so terrified of being uncovered that he would rather allow an epidemic."[93] Kramer concludes his discussion of the play's effect by arguing:

> [F]uture historians will have no choice but to take note. I'm proud of that. I'm proud that I've been able to help gays realize that we who are proud do not have to be victimized by one of our own who is ashamed. Yes, plays can help change history. If you can keep the damn things running.[94]

Whether or not Kramer's claim about Koch is true, he has made some valid points about the impact theater can have. The link between theater and social change need is not a direct, causal one—one that can be measured quantitatively. The impact of such performances can only be determined over time. As Raymond Williams argues in *The Long Revolution*, social change is a process, and each moment of resistance is part of this struggle. The events that occurred in Springfield play a part in this struggle for social change.

A second issue requiring some attention involves what possible benefits these plays have for their immediate audiences. In his article "Mourning and Militancy," Douglas Crimp argues that both strategies are necessary in the fight against AIDS:

> The fact that our militancy may be a means of dangerous denial in no way suggests that activism is unwarranted. There is no question but that we must fight the unspeakable violence we incur from the society in which we find ourselves. But if we understand that violence is able to reap its horrible rewards through the very psychic mechanisms that make us part of this society, then we may also be able to recognize—along with our rage—our terror, our guilt, and our profound sadness. Militancy, of course, then, but mourning too: mourning *and* militancy.[95]

It seems to me that, outside of the Springfield incident, these plays are means through which those not directly affected by the crisis can gain sympathy for those suffering. For the gay community, however, these plays can serve as a way for the community to mourn the loss of an old gay identity based on sexual freedom and mourn the loss of friends and lovers who have died.

Hoffman has acknowledged that, for him, writing *As Is* was a cathartic experience. The play was his "attempt to bring himself back to sanity" and to "humanize" the AIDS issue.[96] And although, as I stated earlier, Hoffman maintains that he did not write a play about AIDS, he has said he "hopes people will come away with sympathy and acknowledgement that research money should be increased."[97] For Larry Kramer, on the other hand, his expressed intention was to get people to act. Kramer explains that he knew he had to write about AIDS and felt that "the play form was the best way to get matters attended to."[98]

As the critical responses to the plays reveal, Hoffman apparently succeeded in humanizing AIDS. For Kramer, however, his expressed goal was not obtained. The controversy surrounding the production of *The Normal Heart* in Springfield did force a number of people to become politically active, but the play itself did not contribute to this activity. As Averback explains:

> Mr. Kramer forcefully delivers his message by focusing on the
> individual, and relying upon that old Aristotelian strategy of
> empathy. The audience empathizes with Ned Weeks and his friends
> through their experiences of love and loss. The audience connects
> to the individual.[99]

But as Augusto Boal argues, "[Aristotle's coercive system of tragedy]
functions to diminish, placate, satisfy, eliminate all that can break the
balance—all, including the revolutionary, transforming impetus."[100]
Averback later observes that it was the mass media's involvement in the
production (which was solely a result of the controversy that arose) that
led some people, including himself, "who were once apolitical," to take
"their first steps towards political activism."[101] Again, this move toward
activism was a result of the controversy that forced the play's entrance
into a "real world" dialogue—an entrance that mainstream theater often
prevents.

In a sense, the Springfield incident could be regarded as unique
because the people who found the production objectionable "misread"
it, intentionally or inadvertently. That is, instead of accepting it as
"drama," they read it as homosexual propaganda. These people placed
the issues into a public forum where those who were involved with the
production and supportive of it were forced to publicly take a stand
regarding the issues raised by those who were opposed to the
production. Hence, the irony of the situation is that the play worked as
Kramer intended only as a result of the response of a community that
did not understand or refused to accept the customary reading position
of mainstream theater audiences. Thus, it could be argued that the play,
in this instance, was successful not because of its ability to resignify
AIDS, but simply because it served as a pretext for promoting some
rather violent discussions and debates about AIDS in a specific
community.

In *Understanding Popular Culture*, John Fiske argues, "The
politics of a cultural form lie in its social mobilizations rather than in
its formal qualities."[102] The incident in Springfield suggests that locating
conservative or radical elements at the level of the text itself, or in
staging conventions/innovations, or in the institution of the theater, or
in that mythical entity "the audience" are not indicative of the political

rhetoric of a play. Fiske concludes, "politics is social, not textual, and if a text is made political, its politicization is effected at its point of entry into the social."[103]

As I have suggested, neither of these plays presents a challenge to the dominant construction of AIDS. AIDS is presented as "a gay disease," a sexually transmitted disease, and, finally, as something that is fatal, which is most apparent at the end of *The Normal Heart* when, after marrying Ned, Felix dies. Such closure, Clum argues, is one element of mainstream gay dramas because, he states, these dramas rarely allow their lovers "to live happily ever after."[104] Additionally, both *The Normal Heart* and *As Is* include a number of elements that are endemic to the traditional theater event, and these elements may prompt the audience to adopt a particular reading formation. Gevisser argues, "In conventional theater both the performers and spectators are unaccountable for their actions: the former because they are 'acting' and the latter because they are, literally, in the dark. Neither performer nor spectator has agency."[105] However, my analysis of these plays and the responses to them suggests that Gevisser's assumption is incorrect. These plays are valuable in terms of promoting discourse in certain situations. As the Springfield example reveals, *The Normal Heart* led to a debate that forced people to become agents, to become active.

But what happens when performances purposively challenge the mainstream theater form—when performances incorporate various reflexive elements in an attempt to differentiate themselves from mainstream theater in order to promote social change? In the next two chapters, the impact of two other forms of performance is explored.

NOTES

1. Shewey xxiii.
2. Gevisser 48.
3. It should be noted that the GMHC is never specifically mentioned in the play. In addition, the word "AIDS" is never uttered in the two hour and forty-five minute play, although it is clear that the "virus," "disease," and "plague" talked about in the play is AIDS.
4. Barnes, "Plague" 12.
5. Kramer, *Just Say No* xvii.
6. Hoffman 105-106.
7. Hoffman 106.
8. Bumbalo 32.
9. Kramer, *Reports* 94. The responses of the critics make it clear that Kramer's play was not viewed as a love story. Perhaps if the play had not appeared almost immediately after *As Is*, *The Normal Heart* might have been read more as Kramer wished; however, because *As Is* centers around the relationship between Saul and Rich, and *The Normal Heart* foregrounds Weeks' conflict with members of the organization, this play was not read as a love story.
10. Kramer, *Normal Heart* 50.
11. Hoffman 15.
12. Hoffman 16.
13. Hoffman 15.
14. Kramer, *Normal Heart* 109.
15. Kramer, *Normal Heart* 35.
16. Kramer, *Normal Heart* 36.
17. Kramer, *Normal Heart* 36.
18. Kramer, *Normal Heart* 109.
19. It should be noted that not all productions of the play have elected to use this technique. When it is included (as it was in the original production and some subsequent productions of the play), it is a powerful reminder of what AIDS is and the impact that it has had. Examples of other Brechtian techniques utilized in each of these plays will be discussed shortly.
20. Kramer, *Normal Heart* 19.

21. The items included during this production are too numerous to include here. See Kramer's play (19-22) for additional examples.

22. Fettner 40.

23. In the production at the Public Theater, the *New York Times'* coverage of the Tylenol scare is compared to its coverage of the AIDS crisis. Although only seven persons were affected by the former, the *Times* published a total of 54 articles about it, four of which appeared on the first page. Only seven articles were written on AIDS in the first nineteen months of the AIDS crisis, although there were 958 reported cases. In the text of the play, the coverage of the AIDS crisis is compared to that of Legionnaire's Disease and toxic shock syndrome. Dr Brookner states that "both hit the front page of the *Times* the minute they happened. And stayed there until somebody did something" (35).

24. Holleran 28.

25. Kramer, *Normal Heart* 57.

26. Kramer, *Reports* 50.

27. Clum 169. The terms in quotations are taken from a lecture on gay literature presented by Eve Sedgwick (ctd. in Clum). Clum adopted these terms from Sedgwick in order to describe the historical impulse.

28. Clum 169.

29. Clum 170.

30. Greif 17.

31. Clum 170.

32. Barnes, "Plague" 12.

33. The other primary message or theme, as I suggested earlier, is that both heterosexual and homosexual institutions are not doing enough to intervene in the crisis.

34. Kramer, *Normal Heart* 57-58.

35. Kramer, *Normal Heart* 60.

36. Clum 187.

37. Kleinberg 30.

38. Kramer, *Normal Heart* 50.

39. Syna 6B.

40. Bumbalo 32.

41. Goldstein, "Kramer's Complaint" 20. Subsequent references to Goldstein in this chapter are from "Kramer's Complaint."

42. Hoffman 15.

43. When *As Is* was revived by the Circle Repertory Company in 1987, Hoffman made a few changes in the script (Merla 29+). In the original production, this scene centered around the first time these characters heard about AIDS. In the revival, the scene focused on the first funeral that people attended, and this is the scene to which the previous comment refers.

44. The scene to which I am referring occurred in 1982, and it was predominantly male homosexuals and IV drug users who were infected with HIV; however, there is no mention of IV drug users anywhere in the play.

45. Hoffman 55.

46. Hoffman 54-55.

47. Gussow 3.

48. Kramer, *Normal Heart* 19.

49. Wright 113.

50. I should note, however, that in *As Is*, the TV announcer does suggest that other populations have been infected: "So far, a vast majority of the cases in this country have been homosexual or bisexual men or intravenous drug users of both sexes, but the disease is beginning to make inroads into the general population" (Hoffman 15).

51. Gevisser 47-48.

52. Gevisser 49.

53. Kramer, *Reports* 92.

54. Bibby 44.

55. His third play about AIDS, *The Destiny of Me*, is a sequel to *The Normal Heart*, and begins in 1992. This play spends significant time addressing issues related to coming out. The play takes place in a hospital room where Ned has come to take part in an experimental drug treatment. Much of the play involves Ned's flashbacks to his youth, his relationship with various family members, and his coming to terms with his homosexuality.

56. Kramer, *Just Say No* xi.

57. Kramer, *Just Say No* xiii.

58. Kramer states that Mel Gussow's review in the *Times* accused the play of being in the worst possible taste" (*Just* xxiii).

59. Henry 85.

60. Kroll 87.

61. Baker 180.

62. Barnes, "Healthy" 50.

63. Shewey xxiv.

64. Fettner 40.

65. Fettner 40.

66. Merla 32.

67. Feingold, Introduction xvi-xvii.

68. Goldstein 20.

69. Kleinberg 29.

70. Clum 187.

71. Kleinberg 30.

72. Hoffman's use of humor also varies from the type of humor Kleinberg and Clum desire. Robert Massa explains, "*As Is* uses humor to stave off sentimentality, but also on occasion to mellow controversy, so overall the characters come off as slightly scrubbed and safe for commercial use" (110). As in *The Normal Heart*, the humor does not reflect the "campy" style often attributed to gay men. Instead, it is a mainstream humor that functions to distance the audience from issues. In *The Normal Heart* the humor, for the most part, appears to diffuse Weeks' anger, at least for the moment.

73. Kleinberg 30.

74. Clum 187.

75. Weales 406.

76. Feingold 50.

77. Feingold xiii-xiv.

78. Gevisser 50.

79. Gevisser 50-51.

80. Gevisser 50-51.

81. Hall 167.

82. Hall 172.

83. Gevisser 48.

84. Gevisser 49.

85. Feingold, Introduction xvi.

86. The information about this controversy was obtained from a panel at the 1990 Speech Communication Association convention entitled, "*The Normal Heart*: A Production in the Face of Adversity. " Unless otherwise noted, the information was taken from Bradley's paper, "The Abnormal Affair of *The Normal Heart*. "

87. The controversy over the SMSU production of *The Normal Heart* occurred at approximately the same time as congressional debates over NEA grants for works considered pornographic.

88. The conflict actually began in the middle of September, 1989, after State Representative Jean Dixon read the play. Dixon called the president of the university to protest the play. During a meeting with the Vice-President and the Dean, Dixon argued for a cancellation of the play or at least editing the parts she found objectionable. Dixon later met with the president of the university who also refused to cancel the production. On October 17, a number of churches condemned the performance and asked parishioners to protest against the play. The final attempt to censor the production occurred at a meeting of the Board of Regents, which coincided with the protest. The Board refused to stop the production, and a week-and-a-half later, the aforementioned advertisement appeared in the newspaper.

89. An article in the *Los Angeles Times* reports that on the same night the director of the production received a call saying "You're next" (Koehler 52). Additionally, Koehler reports that after Evans' house had been destroyed, Donald Trump's secretary called him and said that Trump "wanted to help" (52).

90. Averback 6.

91. Bradley 5.

92. Averback 6.

93. Kramer, *Just Say No* xxii.

94. Kramer, *Just Say No* xxiii.

95. Crimp, "Mourning" 18.

96. Kroll 89.

97. Manischewitz 15.

98. Kramer, *Just Say No* xxii.

99. Averback 4.

100. Boal 47.

101. Averback 6. As I suggested earlier, the reason the university decided to produce *The Normal Heart* was to educate the public about AIDS. However, as Averback explains, the AIDS issue became secondary as issues regarding censorship and the legitimacy of homosexuality were brought to the forefront.

102. Fiske 165.

103. Fiske 168.

104. Clum 176.

105. Gevisser 51.

III

Performance Art:

Karen Finley and Tim Miller

... maybe any function of art ... commerce or spiritualism that
does not basically work in some kind of direction towards healing
the sick ... fostering communication ... easing suffering ...
feeding bodies or saving the planet just ought to get back to the
late 1970s where it would be much more comfortable ...[1]

Whether our code is called abstraction, metaphor appropriation or
inversion. We'll present an image that will affect peoples [sic]
thinking, create images that will take all of the hate and turn it
upside down.[2]

Performance art is a relatively recent phenomenon in the
United States. Although it finds its roots in late 19th/early 20th century
European avant-garde experiments (e.g., Dadaism, Surrealism, and
Futurism), performance art did not become popular in the United States
until the 1970s. According to Henry Sayre, although there were a
number of individuals and groups that led to the development of the
contemporary avant-garde,[3] 1970 "marks the year ... that
'performance' first established itself as a distinct and definable medium
in the feminist arts program run by Judy Chicago and Miriam Shapiro
at Cal Arts in Los Angeles."[4]

The purpose of this chapter is to look at the work of two
performance artists, Karen Finley and Tim Miller, both of whom have
performed texts that deal with the AIDS issue. I am going to pay
particular attention to Finley's *We Keep Our Victims Ready* and Miller's
Stretch Marks as these are the texts I have been able to access. I have
chosen Finley and Miller to represent this form because they are

91

arguably the most famous performance artists who have dealt with AIDS. Their notoriety is primarily due to the refusal by the National Endowment of the Arts (NEA) to grant them funding because, the NEA argued, their work violated its obscenity rule.

The structure of this chapter is somewhat different from the last chapter for a number of reasons. First, because Finley and Miller's notoriety is, in large part, due to the NEA controversy, I present a brief summary of this controversy. Second, because I am dealing with performance art, which is often autobiographical, I also talk about the artists and how their lives have influenced their work. I follow this discussion with a description of their texts. Third, because these texts do not deal solely with AIDS, I pay particular attention to certain segments of the text and place less emphasis to other portions in which other controversial issues are raised.

After a brief explanation of performance art, I summarize the NEA controversy. I then discuss Karen Finley. I present a brief biographical sketch, followed by a summary of *We Keep Our Victims Ready*. Included here is a discussion of Finley's stated and apparent intentions as a performance artist; that is, how she attempts to distinguish her work from theater. I then review the reception of her work and the public persona these responses construct. I conclude my analysis by discussing the implications of her work for social change. The discussion of Tim Miller follows a similar format. I conclude the chapter by comparing and contrasting these performers and their performances, focusing on the issue of social change.

WHAT IS PERFORMANCE ART?

The popularity of new forms of performance resulted from the political climate of the time, most notably the Vietnam War. As Sayre notes, "As a medium, performance was initially intensely political in orientation" and emerged in conjunction with a number of the demonstrations of the late 1960s.[5] The realization that many firms supporting art institutions were also supporting the Vietnam War led many to believe that performance was "one of the better strategies for making art in such overtly politicized times." Art, Sayre explains, needed to be made "objectless"—"uncollectable and unbuyable because intangible."[6] Sayre concludes, "In these terms, art became a useful instrument of change, insofar as its absenting itself as an object undermined the economic and aesthetic norms of the art establishment."[7]

Thus, performance was considered valuable because of its ephemeral quality—a quality that makes it economically subversive. In other words, unlike a painting, for example, which can be bought, sold, and reproduced, no performance can be reproduced. Although a performance can be repeated, subsequent performances are never the same. In an attempt to differentiate itself from drama and to make the performances less commodifiable, performers in the avant-garde tradition often challenged traditional conventions of the theater. As Goldberg explains:

> Unlike theatre, the performer *is* the artist, seldom a character like an actor, and the content rarely follows a traditional plot or narrative. The performance might be a series of intimate gestures or large-scale visual theatre, lasting from a few minutes to many hours; it might be performed only once or repeated several times, with or without a prepared script, spontaneously improvised, or rehearsed over many months.[8]

Michael Heuvel provides additional information regarding the nature and function of performance art, specifically as it is related to the notion of text:

> In its purest form, performance art privileges the spontaneous and physical activity of performing as an autonomous form of artistic expression. That expression is said to differ from literary, textual, or "closed" forms in that it does not impose a preformed hierarchy of discourses or meaning upon the spectator.[9]

A final description of performance art is provided by Bonnie Marranca. Like Goldberg, she also attempts to distinguish performance art from theater:

> Performance art is an anti-theatrical form that displaces illusion with real time, character with personality, skill with spontaneity, artifice with the banal. It values idea over execution; the artist and

> his/her idea is more important than the work itself which has no
> autonomy outside of its creator and the moment of its creation. It
> is a kind of throwaway art that in an odd way links up with the
> cabaret tradition of the classical avant-garde.[10]

In addition to the these qualities, as Heuval suggests, the spectator plays
a different role at a performance art event. Instead of being given the
meaning of the work, the audience has more freedom to interpret it.
This shift, Sayre explains, is from an emphasis on object to
audience—indeed, considerable importance is placed on the audience.[11]
Similarly, Goldberg suggests:

> The history of performance art in the twentieth century is the
> history of a permissive, open-ended medium with endless variables,
> executed by artists impatient with the limitations of more
> established art forms, and determined to take their art directly to
> the public. For this reason its base has always been anarchic.[12]

Hence, the role of the audience and the performer in performance art
differ significantly from their roles in traditional theater. Rather than
passively responding to the event, audiences are engaged more directly
by performance art works in two ways. First, the performers do not take
on a character in the traditional sense; instead, they are presenting
themselves to the audience and address the audience directly. Second,
audiences are ostensibly given more interpretive freedom, as both Sayre
and Heuval suggest.

Another issue to be considered when talking about performance
art involves its reception by critics and academic theorists. As I
suggested above, there are inherent differences between performance art
and theater. However, given its relationship to theater, most notably the
fact that it often occurs in spaces designated as theaters, and its short
history, it is often misread. In other words, many critics do not
understand the nature of performance art. Others are not afforded the
space needed to describe, explain, and evaluate such works. As a result,
they either judge according to traditional theater standards (and often
condemn the work for failing to conform to these standards), they
simply praise the work for dealing with "important social issues," or

they summarize the text, perhaps throwing in a description of a few images created by the performer during his/her performance.

Similarly, there are people, both critics and audience members, who like and appreciate avant-garde forms of performance because they understand the theoretical rationale for postmodern performances. However, often enjoying such performances requires a prior knowledge that many people do not have. Hence, avant-garde performances, such as performance art, often falls prey to charges of elitism.

THE NEA CONTROVERSY

The popularity of performance art has increased since the NEA controversy in 1990. Not only did this controversy lead to larger audiences, but it also increased the number of critical responses addressing these works. The controversy brought performance art out of avant-garde circles and into the awareness of the mainstream population. However, this increase in attention did not, for the most part, create an understanding, either on the part of the critics or mainstream audiences, of performance art. Before discussing these individual performers and their works, I summarize the NEA controversy, for without it, Finley and Miller would probably have remained relatively unknown outside of the performance art world.

The year 1989 probably marks the official beginning of the controversy over funding "obscene" art, for it was during this time that some conservative members of the Congress objected to the funding of photographs by Robert Mapplethorpe and Andres Serrano. Objections to Mapplethorpe's work were raised because his photographs contained "homosexual and sadomasochistic images."[13] Serrano's work drew criticism because of a show that included "Piss Christ," a photograph of a crucifix in a jar of urine. This controversy led to the enactment of an obscenity law, restricting the content of art that receives NEA funding. The law stated:

> Endowment money may not be used for work the agency considers "obscene, including sadomasochism, homoeroticism, the sexual exploitation of children or individuals engaged in sex acts," and

that is not deemed to have "serious literary, artistic, political or
scientific value."[14]

A year later the controversy resurfaced. But, this time objections raised
were against four performance artists.

The controversy began on May 13, 1990, when John
Frohnmayer (chair of the NEA) and the National Council on the Arts
(the advisory board for the NEA) decided to withhold money from 18
solo performance artists recommended for funding by the Solo Theatre
Artist and Mime Panel (composed of theater and performance artists)
until the content of their work had been investigated.

In the middle of June, Frohnmayer asked that the work of
Fleck, Hughes, and Miller be reconsidered by the peer panel. The panel
unanimously voted to fund the 18 artists it had originally recommended.
On June 20, the members of the Council were asked to vote on the
panel's recommendations. They decided to reject the applications of the
three mentioned above and Karen Finley. However, the council did not
announce its decision for another nine days.

On June 27, during a speech in Seattle, Frohnmayer hinted that
"political realities" might force him to veto some of the panel's
suggestions.[15] On June 29, Frohnmayer and the Council announced they
would reject the applications of four of the 18 artists whose work had
been unanimously approved by the peer panel. Frohnmayer justified the
decision by stating that the work of these artists "would not 'enhance
public understanding and appreciation of the arts.'"[16]

The four artists, Karen Finley, John Fleck, Holly Hughes, and
Tim Miller, had all been previous recipients of NEA grants. However,
as Paula Span and Carla Hall explain, the issues they explored in their
work had recently "drawn fire from NEA critics: sexuality (both homo-
and hetero-); nontraditional views of religion; four letter words; attacks
on political and religious antagonists."[17] The four appealed the decision,
but the NEA rejected the appeals, "concluding that there are 'no
grounds on which to entertain reconsideration of the applications.'"[18]
When it was announced that these artists would not receive their grant
money (before their appeal), some artists and institutions decided to
reject the money they were awarded. After their appeal was rejected, the

artists took Frohnmayer to court, arguing that the grounds for the rejection of their applications was political and not artistic.

This controversy resulted in a number of questions regarding standards for art works attempting to receive public funding.[19] For example, when the NEA was reauthorized by Congress for three more years, a "decency clause" was included. (The clause overturned the obscenity law.) The clause stated that the NEA chair must "insure that NEA-funded works adhere to 'general standards of decency and respect for the diverse beliefs and values of the American public.'"[20] And in May of 1992, the acting chair of the NEA, Anne-Imelda Radice, stated that sexually explicit art will have problems getting grant money.[21] The following month, a lawsuit by the "NEA 4" (as they have been subsequently called), struck down the decency clause on grounds that it violated the First and Fifth Amendments of the Constitution.[22]

It is within the context of this controversy that Finley and Miller's works must be viewed. As I suggested earlier, prior to the controversy their works were known mainly within performance art circles. Since this controversy both have gained widespread recognition. In addition, the controversy has certainly affected their work.

KAREN FINLEY: *WE KEEP OUR VICTIMS READY*

Karen Finley was born in Evanston, Illinois, in 1956.[23] Her father, a jazz musician, and her mother, a political activist, instilled in their children a belief in sexual and racial equality, as well as the importance of free speech. During high school Finley began to take courses in performance art at the Art Institute of Chicago. She later entered the San Francisco Art Institute, and eventually received a master's degree in fine arts, specializing in video and performance art.

In 1977, during a school break, her father shot himself in the family's garage. His suicide had a profound effect on Finley's future. She explains:

> It was a violent act. That really put me in such a reality state, of realizing that nothing really ever matters. In some ways, it actually freed me: Whatever you have won't matter. . . Somehow that energy I really put into and show in my work.[24]

After attempting to work through her feelings by painting, Finley turned to performance because of a "need to be with other people."[25] Many of her performance pieces have included segments about her father's suicide. In fact, she claims that the pain she exhibits on stage is a direct result of his death.[26] It was also this experience that led her to appreciate what she calls "real time." In an interview with Richard Schechner, she notes that she dislikes the "show-must-go-on-attitude," and if someone needs her prior to a performance, she will cancel her performance because, she notes, "Someone suffering is always more important than this work."[27]

After a brief stay in Chicago, Finley moved to New York City, where she played in clubs featuring avant-garde performances, such as P.S. 122 and Franklin Furnace. Although she did not receive national attention until the NEA controversy, Finley was used to people having problems with her work. For example, during her first marriage to Brian Routh, her graduate advisor, Finley went to Germany where she and Routh performed a piece that examined the sex lives of Adolph Hitler and Eva Braun. Linn explains that they smeared "chocolate pudding on their buttocks and [got] down on all fours, upon which Finley stuffed wieners and sauerkraut into toy fish and draped them on her body, and Routh sniffed and nibbled at them." Linn records that the audience was so enraged by the performance that they "stormed the stage, shouting, '*We are not like dogs!*'" Another controversial performance was presented in Britain, where she and Routh showed Princess Di as a beautician and Prince Charles as a vendor selling fish-and-chips. As a result of this performance, Finley was asked to leave the country. In response to the event Finley remarked, "They really take their royalty seriously."[28]

In the United States, too, Finley has had to face some harsh audiences. According to Linn, "Skinheads in Miami threw lighted cigarettes at her; the more polite made her dodge pennies. Theaters in Los Angeles, Minneapolis and Miami cancelled her shows because they thought her stuff too controversial."[29]

Prior to the NEA controversy, a performance that sparked a great deal of controversy in the United States was *Yams*, a production that debuted in Los Angeles in 1986. During this performance Finley smeared her body with various foods, including yams. Some claimed that she had stuffed the yams into various orifices, which she claims she never did. A columnist at the *Village Voice* called her performance "vile" (although he had not seen the performance) and suggested that "readers send a yam to his editors, 'who would know what to do with it.'"[30] Interestingly, this controversy increased Finley's following.

In 1987, Finley was going to perform "I'm an Ass-Man," a section of *Yams*, at the Institute for Contemporary Art in London. However, she explains, "I was told by Scotland Yard that I could strip but I couldn't strip and speak at the same time." Coffey explains, "This event, among others, confirmed Finley's belief that it is the power of words that poses the major threat to the dominant culture." It was not until she opened her mouth that she violated Britain's Clause 28, which outlaws activities that appear to promote homosexuality.[31]

Despite these responses abroad and some problems during performances in the United States, Finley had previously acquired NEA grants. Between 1985 and 1987, she received two grants totalling ten-thousand dollars.[32] But on May 11, her 1990 funding became questionable when the *Washington Post* and other papers ran an editorial by Rowland Evans and Robert Novak. Although these columnists had not witnessed her performance of *We Keep Our Victims Ready*, they described her as "a nude, chocolate-smeared young woman" who, if funded by the NEA, could become "the Mapplethorpe case of 1990."[33] Essentially, the article dared the NEA to give her a grant, and Frohnmayer did not accept the dare. Instead, two days later the decision was made to postpone solo performance grant approval. A month-and-a-half later, Finley's application, along with those of Fleck, Hughes, and Miller, was rejected. According to Span and Hall, Finley is probably "the most distraught" of the four about the NEA controversy because, she feels, she "will always now be looked at as the censored artist, the black-listed artist."[34] In a more recent interview with Kirk Fuoss she asserts:

> I've never looked at the attention after the NEA as publicity but more as harassment because it wasn't necessarily about my work. It was from people who had never seen my work. So it didn't

> necessarily serve what I wanted, which was to get the work out. I
> haven't looked at it as something that was positive.[35]

In a number of articles Finley remarks that her work has been greatly
affected by the controversy. Afterward, it took her over a year to create
a new work,[36] and she has had to make changes in the way she
performs.[37] She also claims that the controversy has caused her to lose
bookings, especially if the places in which she is to perform receive
public funding. She summarizes her position rather pessimistically: "I
don't think that fame or celebrity can ever equal injustice."[38]

Karen Finley's *We Keep Our Victims Ready* was first
performed at San Diego's Sushi Gallery in 1989. In the same year, it
was nominated for best play award by the San Diego Theatre Critics.
Since 1989, it has been presented throughout the United States and in
several countries overseas according to a program from one of Finley's
performances. The text is comprised of seven short segments, each of
which focuses on the oppression of various members of society. Finley
has described her performance in this way: "I basically go through
various victims in our society, showing that people are born into
victimization, [into] the patriarchal nature of the society."[39]

Before summarizing the segments of this text, I want to briefly
discuss Finley's performance style. First, Finley uses the written text
during her performance, i.e., her manuscript remains on stage at all
times. Second, her performance does not consist solely of these texts.
She often makes comments that relate to a particular performance
situation and/or audience. Additionally, the images she creates during
her performances are essential to her performances. Third, during her
performances, she often enters a trance-like state and avoids traditional
forms of delivery by chanting the words of the text. Finally, she
presents a number of different personas—sometimes she appears to be
speaking as herself; sometimes she takes on the role of an oppressed
member of society; in other instances, she portrays one who oppresses,
e.g., an abusive male.

My description of Finley's piece is based on the written text
that appears in *Shock Treatment*. Written in poetic form, the text does
not include stage directions or props that Finley uses throughout the
performance. However, in Overn's letter to me he states that the text is

"almost identical" to her performance. He further explains, "Usually in performance, Karen will preface the piece with 'It's Only Art' or, during the Gulf War, with a new piece entitled 'The War at Home.'" "It's Only Art," written prior to the NEA controversy, remarkably foreshadows the NEA controversy of 1990 by dealing with censorship. The first segment of the text, "I Was Not Expected to be Talented," addresses the role of women in contemporary society, especially those who are in lower socioeconomic brackets, and how biology determines what women are allowed to do. The second piece, "Aunt Mandy," is about abortion rights and a woman's freedom to choose. (Aunt Mandy died from an illegal abortion.) The third segment, "St. Valentine's Massacre," focuses on issues of psychological and physical abuse of woman and children.

The next two segments draw comparisons between the world today and other disturbing events in our past and present. In "We are the Oven," Finley compares the events that occurred in Nazi Germany to what is happening in the world today to persons with AIDS, persons of color, homosexuals, and other marginalized members of society. She explains that the lack of attention afforded these people is analogous to what occurred in Nazi Germany, except that "OUR OVENS ARE AT A SLOWER SPEED."[40] From this piece the title of the performance is drawn. And although she mentions AIDS in the previous sections, here she spends significantly more time focusing on the AIDS issue. In the following section, "Why Can't This Veal Calf Walk?," Finley makes an analogy between the life of a veal calf and violence against women in our society.

The final two sections are entitled "Departures" and "The Black Sheep." The first piece examines the death of someone with AIDS. Although AIDS is never mentioned, many of the references she makes suggest that the person has died of AIDS. For example, she refers to her newly deceased character as someone who is young and suggests that there is no way to make him better. The final section of her performance brings together all marginalized members of society, describing them, and Finley herself, under the heading of "Black Sheep." She chooses this label because they are somehow different from the "general population." However, she does not intend for the term

"Black Sheep" to be interpreted in a derogatory way. Instead, for Finley, the term is meant to suggest that these people are part of a larger family. In this section there are references to PWAs and homosexuals, many of whom are rejected by members of their family when they admit to being gay, to having AIDS, and so forth.

Because Finley realizes that performance art is often read as theater, many of the decisions she makes are attempts to break this habitual reading formation in both the critics and her audience. In her interview with Fuoss, Finley denies that she is doing theater because she does not approach her performances as an actress might: "I don't go and do method or something like that."[41] In fact, Finley seems to realize the contradiction involved in performing this piece in the theater:

> Sometimes I even question whether or not I should be doing it in theatres. I look at my work as more conceptual. I appropriated the theatre structure for the work in the same way that Andy Warhol appropriated advertising. I feel like I use the theatrical setting for my own uses.[42]

What Finley implies here is that through her work she is attempting to use the theater against itself in a way similar to Brecht's experiments.

Finley views her performances as rituals or ceremonies, something she feels is lacking in our culture.[43] She does not see herself as a performer in the dramatic mode; instead, she states that she is in a trance when she performs. In an interview with Richard Schechner she states:

> I do go into somewhat of a trance because when I perform I want it to be different than acting. . . . I'm really interested in being a medium, and I have done a lot of psychic type of work. I put myself into a state, for some reason it's important, so that things come in and out of me, I'm almost like a vehicle. And so when I'm talking it's just coming through me.[44]

However, in a her conversation with Fuoss she claims that she has no control over her form of delivery.[45] She has also noted that she never prepares for her performances in the traditional sense; she does not rehearse her performances, nor does she do warm-ups.[46] In her interview with Schechner she admits to being exhausted and to sometimes feeling as though she is going to be physically ill after her performances.[47]

Another way she differentiates herself from traditional theatre is by having her script on stage, even though, as she states in her interview with Fuoss, it does not serve to aid her memory. Instead, she uses a script to "give the performance a certain frame" that "makes it more like a concert." This is a style she expresses some affinity for, something that does not make her seem like a "hysterical" woman who is "out of control."[48]

Thus, each of Finley's choices appear to be conscious attempts to create a particular performance persona—one that makes her seem more credible, and, more importantly, one that differentiates her from a "method" actor. In what follows I discuss the reception of her work, paying particular attention to whether or not she has been successful in creating this persona.

Finley's works have received significant theoretical attention, especially in comparison to Miller's. For example, she is often mentioned in books on feminist performance.[49] But not all of this attention has met with Finley's approval. In a letter from Michael Overn, Finley's manager and husband, he claims that, with the exception of Finley's interview with Richard Schechner, the work that has been published in *The Drama Review* is based on "incorrect facts and assumptions." Overn was referring in particular to an article by Catherine Schuler that was concerned with an earlier work by Finley, *The Constant State of Desire*. Here Schuler argues:

> average spectators, regardless of their gender, are unable to grasp Finley's ideas or understand her objectives—and that this confusion leads inevitably to frustration, anger, and, finally, rejection of her work as a vehicle for meaningful social and political analysis.[50]

Her conclusions are based on an "informal study" after one of Finley's performance, which Finley, in a letter to the editor, called "a public opinion poll gathered in the style of the Folger's Coffee Test."[51] As a result of this article and others by "academicians," Finley admits to being a bit skeptical about their work. In her interview with Fuoss, for example, he asks her about her "uneasy" relationship with academe. She responds, "I question people from academia. This whole performance theory stuff I think a lot of times is crap because it's produced by people who have not created."[52]

The reviews of her work, however, are seemingly more positive, certainly in comparison to Schuler's article. Almost every reviewer applauds her politics and her attempts to get people to see a side of life they often miss. The issues that are consistently raised in the reviews involve her use of images, particularly her nudity, and the relationship between performance art and theater.

A discussion of her use of images is clearly important, as these images are what brought her to the attention of Jesse Helms, Rowland Evans and Robert Novak, and others. (In fact, according to Phelan, it was the article by Evans and Novak in the *Washington Times* that led to Finley's rejection by the NEA.[53]) Every article discusses the smearing of chocolate on her "naked" body; however, the difference between the understanding of this act by the reviewers and conservatives (many of whom have never seen her perform) is that the reviewers suggest that the nudity is neither pornographic nor erotic. Maria Nadotti explains:

> The nudity, the talk-dirty language, the "perverse" treatment of the body—there are obvious parallels here between Finley's work and conventional pornography. But the two are in fact quite unlike. It's not just the strength of Finley's stage persona—she's no one's play thing—or the vigor and resourcefulness of her writing, or the incantatory yet suspenseful inflections of her voice, sometimes breaking down into pure noise, that distinguish her performances from the objectified, fragmented eroticism of porno. Finley magnifies—overexposes—exhibitionism to the point where it is deeroticized.[54]

For Nadotti, Finley's nudity is not pornographic because it helps the audience understand how a woman's body is objectified by men. In effect, what Nadotti suggests is that Finley subverts the male gaze. And although Nadotti is making a statement about Finley's performances in general, her argument certainly applies to *We Keep Our Victims Ready*.

The issue of subverting the male gaze is a complicated one. Briefly stated, "the male gaze" was coined by Laura Mulvey to describe how films are constructed to please male viewers—that they replicate gender differences in society in which men are active and women are passive.[55] In relation to this particular performance, Finley's subversion of this gaze is arguably accomplished through her attempts to make her nudity non-sexual and non-pornographic. In other words, by smearing chocolate on her body, which, in the context of her performance signifies excrement, Finley challenges the view of women as sexual objects.[56]

In his review of a performance in San Diego, Charles Wilmoth notes that the objectification of women by men is one of Finley's primary concerns. Somewhere in the middle of the performance Finley uses the food that has made her so famous. She removes all of her clothes except her panties. She then covers her body with chocolate, followed by alfalfa sprouts and tinsel. The chocolate represents excrement, the sprouts, sperm. The tinsel adds a sense of taste that is expected of women by men in society. (In some performances she has also used sprinkles and candy hearts.) When she finishes applying these items, she appears to be wearing a cocktail dress.[57] This image, Finley claims, expresses "the condition of women"—"covered with excrement, phony sugar romance and sperm under a glittering patina of illusion called 'desirability.'"[58]

All the reviews devote some space to talking about this now infamous image in Finley's performance. Additionally, and unlike many of the reviews for other performances, the criticism of her work is largely descriptive. Outside of praising her, as most do, for her commitment to social issues, the critics spend a great deal of time summarizing her performances and interpreting some of her images. The evaluative element of the criticism, as I suggested, praises her enthusiasm and commitment, and talks about the impact that her performances can potentially have on the audience. However, as I have argued, the praise is largely due to the issues she raises rather than the performance itself, an approach, like a heavy reliance on description, that is not specific to Finley but endemic to reviews of performance art in general.

One other element that is found in almost all of these critiques is a description (and sometimes a history) of performance art, especially as it distinguishes itself from theater. Like the general descriptiveness of the reviews, these distinctions seem to aid the audience in understanding this lesser-known art form. For example, Kay Larson explains:

> Performance art is the least understood of the genres. It may look like theater, but its practitioners are usually artists who easily slip back and forth between visual forms and live action. . . . The distinction between performance art and theater is delicate but crucial. Artists of the sixties rejected the traditional theatrical process of projecting themselves into a role written by someone else. They resist having to erase their personalities in order to assume another.[59]

By providing such distinctions these reviewers are trying to help their audiences understand what they are about to witness. And, in other ways, by describing performance art, they are also helping the audience members decide whether or not they want to witness these "non-traditional" performances. But these distinctions may also help explain why the praise of Finley's work is due to her subject matter as opposed to her performance—it is virtually impossible to explain what performance art is in the amount of space available to most reviewers. Consequently, many theater critics focus on the subject matter of the performance to avoid having to deal with the theoretical baggage associated with performance art.

What I find most interesting about Finley's reviews is that they are obviously directed towards the mainstream theater audience—not performance art patrons. Persons familiar with the performance art scene obviously understand its history, or at least they know something about it. Yet, it seems these reviewers felt a need to provide background into performance art, regardless of the context in which their articles appear. These descriptions appear in a wide variety of magazines and newspapers, even in those published in cities where performance art has been going on for a number of years (e.g., New York City and Los Angeles). While I hesitate to suggest that these highly descriptive explanations about performance art are solely a result of the NEA controversy, the controversy clearly has played a role in this decision. As I remarked earlier, the NEA controversy made the term "performance art" familiar to people who had little or no knowledge about this particular art form, some of whom were inspired to see these performances. Perhaps as a means to prepare them for the works, or perhaps to help them contextualize these works after seeing them, reviewers seem to feel the need to explain what performance art is. And perhaps their research into the performance art tradition is an attempt to help them understand this particular art form.

Two other essays take a different approach to categorizing Finley's work by suggesting how her performances differ from stereotypical performance art, if there is such a thing, and theater. For example, Luc Sante's review states that Finley "establishes an easy rapport with the audience—a rare thing in performance art, where the tone often tends toward the chilly, the arch, or the adversarial."[60] In another review, Feingold notes that he often avoids performance art because the "art gets buried in an abstract wash of self-indulgent impulses."[61] For Finley, though, he has quite a different response. He seems to suggest that because she is not self-indulgent (which I read as his own aversion to works that are autobiographical), she is justified in what she is doing. She becomes the scapegoat for all of society's "victims," which, Feingold argues, makes her work "inevitable" and important.[62]

Of course, not all the responses to Finley's work are positive, but only three of these reviews are clearly negative.[63] And sometimes the negative responses often result from the theatrical frame that many critics use to judge her work. In what follows I present some of the negative criticism Finley has received.

Village Voice critic Jonathan Kalb, in his overtly negative critique, condemns Finley for working too hard "to keep her soul honest and her art dangerous." Viewing her performance in the context of the NEA controversy, Kalb distinguishes this performance from her other performances. He explains that she does not appear to concentrate as much on her texts as she has in the past. Unlike other reviewers who praise her for the rapport she creates with the audience, Kalb objects:

> [S]he interrupts (and *distracts*) herself repeatedly in order to issue half-hearted chastisements to spectators—"You can read the program after the show" and makes pissy, pseudopersonal cracks about "any rich cooters out there" and "any dramaturgs among you."

He continues to berate Finley for ejecting someone from the audience for coughing and says "her misplaced prima donna act has utterly alienated the audience." He supports his point by quoting a female member of the audience who was in the lobby after the performance: "Lady, you're just as much a fucking fascist as any of those fucking people you're talking about."[64]

Kalb's critique lacks specificity and differs greatly from the other reviews that find flaws in Finley's performance. He mentions few elements of the performance itself, except for the aforementioned interruptions and seems to suggest that the performance had no redeeming quality whatsoever. Other negative responses to her performance seem more credible to me in that they do not reject the entire performance; instead they suggest that there are some problems with it.

Sante's problems center around what he sees as "unsophisticated and lazy" thinking and writing on Finley's part.[65] Another of Sante's objections involves the metaphors she uses. He claims she is uncomfortable with both these metaphors and language in general, and uses the comparison she draws between the Holocaust and the United States today as an example of her "hollow rhetoric." He further claims that the fascist metaphor has been so overused that "it is now all but meaningless."[66] While I do not feel this is the place to challenge all of Sante's criticisms, I do find Finley's use of the Holocaust metaphor extremely powerful in this context. Perhaps the Holocaust metaphor has been overused in relation to the AIDS crisis. (As I noted in the previous chapter, both Kramer and Hoffman use this metaphor at points in their plays.) Yet, the metaphor seems quite appropriate based on the inattention various institutions give to the crisis. In fairness to Sante, he does say there are some similarities between the two; however, he argues that the overusage of the Holocaust metaphor has forced it to lose its power.

Finally, Sante asserts that because her words rely so heavily on other words within her text, "it is almost impossible to quote" and that the impact of these words can only be grasped in the context of her performance.[67] Although it could be argued that this final comment could be construed as a compliment, in the context of the review it is clearly negative. Sante clearly does not approve of many of the elements in Finley's performance.

Sante's objections to Finley's performance seem to stem largely from the classic realist standards he applies to this postmodern performance. For example, he argues that the spontaneity of her performance (which he refers to as "a fear of too much polishing") is "the hallmark of her artistic generation." But such spontaneity is part of performance art. It is a means through which the performance does not allow itself to be repeated, thereby resisting its commodification. Additionally, while he seems to condemn Finley for the important role the performance of her texts play, I do not feel Finley would view such a response as a criticism. Again, Sante seems to condemn her performance based on traditional theatrical standards because, he argues, the text itself does not stand on its own. Sante concludes his review by praising her performance, in spite of its faults: "It is easy to misrepresent her work, but impossible to duplicate it."[68] This final comment can be viewed as an apology for what he has said because I would argue, and I think Finley would agree, that he has, in some instances, misrepresented her work.[69]

Gretchen Faust also finds fault in some of Finley's choices. However, unlike Sante, she believes Finley's work maintains a traditional theatrical device that performance art supposedly has relinquished—catharsis. For Faust, Finley's "stream-of-political/social-consciousness screaming necessarily dictates the role of art as cathartic." As performance art attempts to differentiate itself from the emotional involvement and response encouraged by realistic performances, evoking this model allows Faust to talk about (and condemn) Finley's performance. However, Faust's comment suggests that Finley's performance is not a cathartic experience for the audience; instead, it is a cathartic experience for herself. Additionally, Faust closes off any other interpretation of the work by insisting that such an approach "dictates" reading the work as cathartic. She later claims that Finley's "comments imply an 'us-vs.-them' polarity that does little to promote a kind of atmosphere that results in a real grasp of the issues involved."[70] Thus, Faust appears to condemn Finley for benefiting from her performance, seemingly suggesting that it is okay for the audience to have a cathartic experience, but not the performer.

Laura Jacobs' response to Finley's work levels a similar charge. She explains that the aggressiveness of the performance is its weakness:

> Finley never moves beyond confrontational complaint. Her show is static, the theatrical equivalent of a sit-in (and not merely because she is always sitting). The food is forced to do all the visual work. It is an adequate device for demonstrating self-love and hate, sexual pleasure and abuse—but that's all it is, a device.

This "confrontational complaint," Jacobs claims, "will not change your mind" if you disagree with her views, and if you agree with her, "the performance is a depressing reading of woes, utterly lacking in cleverness." She concludes her discussion of the performance by quoting the response of a friend: "The thing she has going for her is that things stick to chocolate."[71]

Jacobs' critique of Finley is clearly negative. Her tone throughout the review is overtly sarcastic, which, in and of itself, is not problematic. However, Jacobs obviously did not check her facts, choosing to base some of her "insight" into Finley's performances on incorrect information. Additionally, she seems to exhibit a rather negative attitude towards performance art and Finley herself. She tells us she went to see the show because of all the publicity and claims that Finley takes advantage of the NEA controversy by using "It's Only Art" as her opening piece, using it to ingratiate herself with or build support from her audience. She describes Finley's "rhetorical style" after the opening piece as recalling "the snake-oil sensuality of a TV evangelist."[72]

Jacobs' review could be read as an "I-don't-see-what-the-big-deal-is" response to Finley's performance. However, her negativity towards almost every aspect of the performance suggests that while she does not understand why the performance has raised so much controversy (suggesting, in part, that the reason for this is that "almost anything goes" in performance art), she negates the message that Finley is trying to get across. Like Kalb, she seems to have little use for the message that Finley wishes to convey and for performance art in general.

Finally, Margaret Spillane's review deserves some attention. Unlike the other critics who pan Finley's performance, Spillane argues that Finley seems to exploit the subject of the performance:

> The truly unpleasant surprise about Finley's performance was its utterly conventional treatment of her subject matter. All the controversy seemed to promise a bare-knuckled assault on those barriers separating the privileged from the powerless. . . . The individual victims she promised to evoke—the battered child, the exploited female service worker, the person with AIDS—turned out to be carelessly assembled amalgams of bourgeois Americans' cultural shorthand for those they believe exist beneath them.

Spillane's problem with Finley's performance is that she and the other artists who were denied funding all fail to answer important questions that are at the core of the controversy: "Who gets to make art; who even gets to imagine that they might become an artist? And who gets to have their story told through art?" Hence, Spillane believes these artists need to understand that although they are members of marginalized groups, they are all privileged. She argues that Finley and the others must recognize that the NEA controversy is not only about the censorship of art by conservatives; it is also about the artist's complicity in the system that perpetuates these crimes. In other words, Spillane's point is that the people Finley wants to present her works to are precisely those people who create the injustices Finley and the others are fighting against.[73] Finley and the others are privileged in that they are allowed to speak for the "victims" of society, while the "victims" are still not permitted to speak for themselves.

Spillane raises some interesting questions regarding the public funding of art. She suggests that those artists working for social change and accepting public money are participating in the system that keeps these "victims" in their place. Although Spillane fails to mention that it is possible to work within the system of oppression to change it, she does make some important points regarding those artists who are supported by public funds. For they too, she argues, are engaging in a form of censorship. According to Spillane, Finley "is emblematic of the art-making population's troublingly restricted notion of who its audience needs to be, and its equally troubling lack of alarm at who is being entirely left out of the art-making, -consuming and -rewarding tracks."[74] Unlike the majority of reviewers on Finley that praise her for addressing such significant issues, Spillane raises some important and interesting questions about the nature and function of art in our times.

TIM MILLER: *STRETCH MARKS*

Prior to the NEA controversy few comparisons would have been drawn between Tim Miller and Karen Finley, except for the fact that they are both performance artists. Miller was born in Whittier, California—the hometown of Richard Nixon—in 1958.[75] Unlike Finley's family, Miller's was conservative. However, Miller would certainly not be included in the conservative category. Miller is openly homosexual and a staunch AIDS activist.

In 1978, when Miller was 19, he left California for New York City. Having developed a strong interest in solo performance during high school, Miller was interested in the performance art scene that was emerging in the city, a place where he could "do the big white man postmodern art dance thing."[76] While in New York he took classes and tried to make it in performance. However, during this time he realized that many of the major gay artists remained secretive about their sexual orientation. Miller admits, "I felt really betrayed at that time by this whole generation of artists who managed to be living in the '60s and '70s—a period of ferment for gay people—and didn't manage to lift a finger."[77] Partly in response to this belief, Miller co-founded P.S. 122 in 1980, a performance space dedicated to alternative work. Shortly thereafter he arranged a festival featuring performance art by gay artists.

In 1986, Miller returned to California with his lover, feeling more comfortable in Los Angeles because the community was much more politicized. Three years later, in 1989, Miller, with Linda Frye Burnham (founder of *High Performance Magazine*), created Highways, a performance space dedicated to presenting socially conscious works.

In addition to Miller's strong involvement with ACT UP (for which he has created works that explore the relationship between art and society), he collaborates with an openly-gay Episcopal priest, Malcolm Boyd, presenting "performance art sermons," which have sparked some controversy.[78] He has been arrested numerous times, once for his involvement with a guerilla theater performance that "convicted the government of crimes against the First Amendment."[79] He has also taught performance courses at UCLA.

Miller's performance art work and his other activities are very much intertwined. As Breslauer explains, "The way Miller assesses value . . . is inextricably tied to his activist stand, but it's also with a feel for where the vitality is in the art world at the moment." In the same article Miller is quoted as saying, "The most interesting work is coming out of communities of crisis; it's a deep cultural call. . . . It makes people come to the work in a charged way."[80]

Miller's response to the rejection of his grant application was anger. In fact, he and some members of ACT UP later confronted Frohnmayer during a speech he was giving in Atlanta. Five security guards had to remove Miller from the room. In the process, they ripped his shirt. Miller claims that this physical act on the part of the guards "made an impression on people—many of whom had watched me perform the night before—to see an artist manhandled and dragged out of the presence of the head of the federal agency."[81] A couple of years later, during another of Frohnmayer's speeches, Miller confronted him again, accusing Frohnmayer of lying to the audience by insisting that his and the other three applications were *not* rejected because of political reasons.

Miller's *Stretch Marks* deals most obviously with homophobia and AIDS, although he mentions other social issues throughout the performance (e.g., the Tiananmen Square massacre). The piece is clearly autobiographical in that it centers on events that have happened to him during his life. At the beginning of the performance, he tells us he is waiting for a train to come while standing on a beach, and he begins to reminisce about what the beach has meant to him throughout his life. Shortly thereafter he speaks of his fear of flying, even though he must fly on occasion. He explains that he hates flying because a close friend and fellow performance artist was killed in the terrorist bombing of Pan Am Flight 103. This is why, he tells us, he takes the train.

Miller then discusses a trip he took around the United States, the people he met, and the places he saw. In recounting this trip, he also explains different events that have occurred throughout his life. The train serves as a metaphor through which he can re-experience his past. On the train he takes us from his childhood to the present (although not necessarily in chronological order). He tells us, for example, about the lesbian Chicano who taught him German in High School, the politics of his hometown, and getting sick on his twenty-ninth birthday (which is juxtaposed with the song "Climb Every Mountain" from *The Sound of Music*). He also reenacts a performance he gave during an ACT UP demonstration that took place at the Los Angeles County General Hospital in January of 1989. The demonstration was aimed at getting more programs and facilities for PWAs. This hospital was selected, Miller tells us, because it is the largest in the world and does not have an AIDS unit.

His performance/speech he presents during the demonstration soon evolves into a list of "maybes," which are his hopes for the future, followed by his reasons for wanting these things to happen—his "becauses." Here he touches on everything from the function of art to gay and lesbian rights. His speech ends and he is back on the train reminiscing. He soon begins the story that ends the performance. The story is about the people with whom he once ate a meal on a train; however, it is a story, he claims, about the stories the people told him. He did not share a story with these people, but concludes the piece by sharing the story he would have told. His story is about a train graveyard he used to play in as a child and recently visited as an adult. The "dead" trains remind him of people (both living and dead) who have either been a part of his life or have had some impact on it. At the end, he is on a train that is carrying him, the others he has seen in the graveyard, and everyone else to the beach.

The reviews of Tim Miller's *Stretch Marks* are easily summarized because I could locate only two. Three issues stand out in these reviews, especially when they are compared to those of Finley. First, issues surrounding the history and nature of performance art are not as predominant in these reviews, including those that are not of this particular performance. Second, by comparison, Miller has received significantly less attention than Finley. Third, every review mentions the fact that Miller's performances deal with his sexuality, homophobia, and AIDS.

All of these issues are arguably interrelated. Because his performance addresses homosexuality and AIDS, one might suggest that he gets less coverage by the mainstream press, which could explain the relatively small amount of information available on his performances. Additionally, it could be argued that the nature of performance art does not have to be explained by these critics because they assume that it is not the genre that will attract the audience, it is, in fact, the subject matter itself. In comparison to Finley, it is unlikely that people will go see Miller perform if they want to learn about performance art. The subject matter overwhelms the type of artistic expression in which Miller is engaged.

The fact that his work deals with sex and AIDS makes his performances less accessible to mainstream audiences, according to some reviewers. For example, one reviewer explains:

> Miller makes it clear that he assumes his audience is almost entirely gay and that assumption colors his language. Many who are not gay will find his descriptions of homosexual acts and the context of the nude scene offensive or, at the least, discomforting.[82]

While Keating refers specifically to Miller's *Sex/Love/Stories*, such a claim could be made about *Stretch Marks* (although Miller never takes off his clothes in this performance).[83] Regardless of his message, the depiction of homosexuality in the performance receives top billing, especially in mainstream presses. Keating ends his review by saying that the "discomfort is worth risking" because "Miller has something to say, and he says it with passion and theatricality."[84] However, it seems very unlikely that those who do not accept Miller's views will choose to attend his performance.

The reviews of *Stretch Marks* are from relatively liberal presses and are both short (a page or less). The first review, by Jowitt, comes from the *Village Voice* and is purely descriptive. Essentially, her review is a one-page summary of his performance with a call to see the performance at the end. She seems especially intrigued by Miller's train metaphor: "[T]his is the train all of us are riding. All aboard?"[85] Due to the nature of her review, Jowitt does not overemphasize the homosexuality and AIDS issue. She avoids this by refusing to present a brief, overarching summary of the work.

The second review, by Mygatt, is included in *Backstage*. In this review, Mygatt briefly describes Miller's relationship to performance art and notes that this performance "is both a deeply personal exploration and a strong political statement." He then mentions how Miller uses some of his props and concludes the review by discussing Miller's involvement in ACT UP, pointing out that *Stretch Marks* includes a piece Miller performed at one of ACT UP's demonstrations, and claiming that this is "one of the piece's strongest moments." (While performing this segment, Miller climbs on a soap box.) Mygatt concludes that Miller's performance is about "one man's confrontation with his own mortality," and "it is also the story of our times." [86] Like Jowitt, Mygatt impresses upon the reader the importance of the work that Miller is doing; however, he personalizes the issue for Miller, failing to mention the importance that the issue has for all of us, as Jowitt attempts to do. In spite of his references to Miller's activism, Mygatt stresses the impact that Miller's "fear of death" has for him and, to some extent, pats him on the back for continuing to cope with the struggle.

COMPARISONS AND CONCLUSIONS

To conclude this chapter, I compare and contrast these performances. Rather than discussing all the similarities and differences between their works, I focus primarily on those issues that relate to their political effectiveness. I begin by focusing on their texts and performances, ending with a discussion of how they address the AIDS issue. I then compare their critical responses. I conclude this section by discussing how the conventions of mainstream theater may, in a more general sense, impact the efficacy of their work.

The primary similarity between these texts is that both deal with oppressed members of society. However, while Finley looks at a variety of groups, Miller spends most of his time talking about homophobia and AIDS. Additionally, both talk about the role of art in contemporary society. Finley, though, is more concerned with government censorship while Miller spends his time talking about the political function of art (as the introductory quote by him at the beginning of this chapter suggests).

More importantly both performers argue that they are using their works as a means to promote social change. For example, Finley is quoted as saying, "I do things for a hopeful reason. . . . I do them because I want to effect change."[87] Miller, challenging traditional, modernist conceptions of art, maintains that the importance of a work of art is not its quality, but whether it "changes how we understand the world," if it "opens a window for people to see another part of our city."[88] As the title of Breslauer's article reveals, for Miller, art is equal to activism. In another essay Miller maintains, "I think art can change the way people view the world. I think art can also change the world itself."[89]

The main difference between their texts is a result of the way they approach performance art. As I suggested earlier, Miller's works are autobiographical. His text for *Stretch Marks* talks about a number of experiences he has had in his life. Finley, on the other hand, uses her experience as a woman to understand the oppression of various groups in society. While some of her "stories" may be true, by comparison many of the texts she includes in *We Keep Our Victims Ready* include different personas she takes on throughout. In this sense, her work leans more towards taking on roles, in a traditional sense, than Miller's. Finley would most likely reject this view of her performance; however, such a description best differentiates her from Miller.

Finley has also objected to questions regarding whether or not her work is autobiographical, whether she has ever experienced what she discusses in her performance. In Linn's article she is quoted as saying:

> You wouldn't believe how many people come right out and ask me if I've been raped. No one asks Martin Scorsese if he's murdered someone. No one asks David Lynch if he tortures women. And I don't know, it strikes me, first—why does it matter? And then I

think, if I say yes, what would yes mean? I think it would diminish
my work.[90]

Miller does not appear to hold the same opinion regarding his work. In
other words, I do not believe he would argue that the autobiographical
nature of his work diminishes either its content or impact.

Another difference between these two performers is the way
they deal with their audiences, that is, the relationship they attempt to
create. One similarity between the two is that they both address the
audience, something that is commonplace in performance art. But Finley
creates a very different relationship with her audience. In her interview
with Fuoss she observes, "I am very kind to the audience."[91] And in
some ways she is. Linn describes her as "chatty and charming, almost
Betty Boopish."[92] She establishes a very friendly atmosphere at the
beginning of her performance by having a one-way conversation with
the audience while sitting in a rocking chair. However, she also could
be charged with lulling the audience into a false sense of security.
Sometimes she outwardly confronts and even assaults the audience as
a whole and sometimes she selects specific members of the audience.
And her frequent use of the second person alternates between being
accusatory and comforting.

This is not to say that her use of the pronoun "you" refers
specifically to the audience. In fact, except when she uses the term "you
see," the "you" seems to refer to an unseen male. However, it is
possible for the audience to read themselves into the "you." I find her
use of the term "you" an interesting rhetorical choice because when she
uses the term, she is usually referring to a male. (Sometimes it seems
to refer to society in general.) If she had used the term "he" instead of
"you," the target of her discourse would be less ambiguous. The
ambiguity of the term, I would maintain, gives the performance more
rhetorical power because it could be argued that the term affords the
audience less distance, perhaps implicating them as part of the
problem.[93]

For example, sometimes the "you" is a person who is
physically or emotionally abusive, like the "you" she refers to at one
point in "I Was Not Expected to be Talented." She explains, "And when
I see you / after you beat me / after you degrade me / and you stand on

top of me / in some god-awful museum / you say to me, / There are no great women artists!"[94] In "Departures," on the other hand, the "you" she refers to is the lover of the person who is about to die of AIDS. If the audience chooses to see themselves in this role they will probably feel more comfortable than they would in the previous example. However, the homosexual implications in the performance may make some people, heterosexual men for example, extremely uncomfortable.

Unlike Finley, Miller appears more distanced from his audience, appearing to save his confrontations for his involvement with ACT UP, although not necessarily during the performance works he presents in the context of these demonstrations. For example, when he recreates his performance at the ACT UP demonstration at the Los Angeles hospital, it becomes clear that, in its original context, the performance was designed to inspire fellow activists. When he reenacts the work in *Stretch Marks*, his preface to it seems to distance the audience from the inspirational intention it had in its original context. He clearly sets it up as a performance, in a more traditional sense, within his larger performance of *Stretch Marks*:

> There is a performance area right here. A stage. And these are my props. This is the ACT UP/LA week-long vigil in front of County Hospital to protest the lousy care PWA's . . . are getting in this city. . . . This is the closing rally. There have been performances and readings and music. Now it's my turn. I come out from the group, approach the stage and begin.[95]

Miller's subtext says to the audience "I am going to perform for you." In some ways this frame differentiates or delineates what he said before and what occurs after this scene from particular segments of the performance. By clearly setting this segment up as a performance, he does not force the audience into a different role than they previously played. That is, he does not turn them into members of ACT UP. It could be argued that his choice to preface this segment helps them remain comfortable with the performance, especially if they do not approve of ACT UP's tactics. They have a choice—to place themselves in the role of ACT UP members or to remain as part of the audience of the larger work.

In his interview with Burnham, Miller talks about ACT UP and its radicalism. He states, the tactics they engage in

> are so consistent with the history of the avant-garde, of shocking the bourgeoisie. Except now you actually do it, you don't pretend to do it by being in coffeehouses. You actually go to the halls of justice and law and power and confront them on their turf, not in dada cafes.[96]

Such radicalism does not appear to play a role in his performance art work. However, it is interesting to note that he argues what ACT UP does is "pure performance" because it challenges, exposes dishonesty, lies and contradictions.[97]

Like Finley, Miller uses the personal pronoun "I" quite often. But unlike Finley, the "I" he refers to is clearly himself. He is talking about the events that have occurred in his life. When Finley uses "I" she is not always referring to herself, since we see her as different "I's" throughout the performance. Sometimes she is a woman who has been raped, as in "I Was Not Expected to be Talented"; sometimes she is an abusive male, as in "St. Valentine's Massacre"; and sometimes we get the impression that the "I" refers to an event she has actually experienced, as in "Departures."

In Miller's performance we never doubt that he is referring to himself when he uses the first person. His rapport with the audience differs from Finley's in that his relationship with them remains consistent throughout the performance. The fact that he is disclosing to them may make the audience feel a certain degree of closeness, comfort, sympathy or empathy; however, it is unlikely that their feelings will waver a great deal throughout the performance as a result of his interaction with them. This is not to say that the audience will remain entirely comfortable—they may feel uneasy, for example, during particular parts of the performance. But these feelings are most likely to be a result of *what* he says (i.e., the content) rather than *how* he says it (i.e., self-disclosure) because the "how" remains relatively consistent throughout. In other words, he continuously uses the first person; unlike Finley, he does not alternate his pronouns throughout the performance. Miller interpellates the audience in a consistent relationship with his discourse. Autobiographical tendencies in performance artists are rather common. As Thomas Mygatt explains, "there is something undeniably fascinating about hearing people expose intimate details about themselves." He goes on to imply that the connection created between the performer and audience "can have tremendous power."[98]

Two other, less significant, differences can be found in these performances. First, Finley never physically enters the audience. Miller does. Immediately after the ACT UP scene Miller suspends himself over the audience. Secondly, after he climbs down from the rafters he solicits the assistance of some audience members in providing lighting for the end of the performance. After he climbs down from the rafters he screams for the lights to be turned out and hands flashlights to some of the audience members who help him remain visible.

Both Finley and Miller are successful, at least in terms of their textual content, in challenging the dominant construction of AIDS, or, at least, refraining from being complicitous in this dominant construction. Here we find some differences between these performances and the plays discussed in the previous chapter. However, because Miller is gay and addresses AIDS and homosexuality in his performance, it may be difficult to disassociate the two. Additionally, the importance of providing support for persons with AIDS is the focus of the most detailed AIDS section of his work.

AIDS has had a profound impact on Miller's life. Although he is not HIV-positive, the loss of a number of friends has made the AIDS crisis a top priority in his performances and his personal life. Miller's first specific reference to AIDS appears approximately halfway through his performance when he remembers taking a train from a memorial service for a friend. The AIDS issue arises again when he begins to repeat the performance he enacted at the hospital demonstration. Miller does not mention specific friends who have died. Instead, he talks about people who do not have health insurance and need good treatment—not the kind that they receive in public hospitals. Although he does not come right out and say it, he seems to construct the AIDS issue as something like a war that is being waged against people who, for some reason or another, are not allowed to participate in the "American Dream"— those who are not allowed to reap the benefits afforded to people who are financially stable. The AIDS issue surfaces again towards the end of the performance when he speaks of his "friends and lovers dead from AIDS."[99]

In the context of the demonstration, AIDS does not carry the baggage that has been placed on it by the dominant discourse, largely because of the context in which the speech occurs and the audience he is addressing. But when he mentions his friends and lovers, he does, given his own sexual orientation, link AIDS and homosexuality. However, I do not think it can be argued, given the brevity of these references, that they should be viewed as perpetuating this link. The link is most apparent in the fact that he is gay and devotes some of his performance to the AIDS issue.

Finley escapes this trap that is unavoidable for Miller. That is, because heterosexual females are considered more distanced from AIDS, Finley is better able to create a distinction between homosexuals and AIDS, and to resignify what AIDS means. Her initial references to AIDS are found in the first two segments of *We Keep Our Victims Ready*. In these references, Finley implies that God must be dead because he would not allow people to suffer and die from AIDS if he were alive. AIDS reappears in the third section, "St. Valentine's Massacre," when she talks about children who die from AIDS due to the neglect of many dominant institutions. Although she mentions many "forms of death," AIDS appears in her list three times and is referred to when she mentions that "no free needles" are distributed.

In "We are the Oven" Finley makes her most explicit references to AIDS. After summarizing the events that occurred in Nazi Germany, Finley talks about the United States today. She begins by charging, "Many people think that junkies and people with AIDS deserve to die."[100] In this sentence Finley refuses to link people who use drugs with AIDS—she does not imply here that drug users are persons with AIDS and that persons with AIDS are drug users. For her, these are two separate categories. She uses the same strategy towards the end of this section when she states, "Some folks who call themselves Christians / Would like to put all homosexuals and people with / AIDS in concentration camps."[101] Again, she fails to place homosexuals and

PWAs in the same category, choosing instead to suggest that while they are treated similarly, the two are not the same.

Another AIDS reference comes shortly after her statement about drug abusers. Here, she condemns those who believe that people who are HIV-positive should be "branded like those in concentration camps," or that providing people with clean needles is "giving them the wrong message."[102] While such a statement recognizes that the virus can be transmitted through dirty needles, it does not equate AIDS and IV drug use.

While AIDS is not mentioned in "Why Can't This Veal Calf Walk?" it is featured in "Departures." In this section, Finley is clearly referring to a gay man who is dying from AIDS. But she uses this person to represent all people who have died by speaking of those who are left behind in terms that refer to both heterosexual and homosexual relationships. She uses the terms "widower," "widow," "friend," and "lover" to describe the people who are affected by someone who has died. AIDS is never specifically mentioned here. But, as I suggested earlier, the less-than-subtle references imply that the person has AIDS. This section is about love and loss. And regardless of the reason the person died, Finley suggests the feelings experienced by his friends and family are universal. In short, Finley's rhetoric is designed to downplay the stigma of death-from-AIDS by intensifying its similarity to death-in-general.

In the final section of the performance, "The Black Sheep," Finley again refuses to refer specifically to AIDS. Instead, she brings all the oppressed people she has mentioned throughout the performance into the "Black Sheep" category. Her references to the relationship between these people and their families are not specific to homosexuals, persons with AIDS, or any of the other marginalized people she has previously mentioned. Although some of her references can be read as references to PWAs, they can also be considered as more "generic" references to anyone who may not fit into the category of "average" citizen (as if there is such a thing). For example, at one point she asserts, "Sometimes Black Sheep are chosen to be sick / so families can finally come together and say / I love you."[103] While it would be easy to read this statement as an indication that the "sick" person has AIDS, such a connection would negate the fact that any illness can potentially bring families together. In this work Finley seems to imply a commonality between all people who are marginalized—women, homosexuals, PWAs, etc.—without perpetuating any of the stereotypes that exist.

Thus, both Miller and Finley do not perpetuate the dominant construction of AIDS. They do not, on the other hand, overtly challenge this construction. Yet, their refusal to make links that allow these narratives to be continued suggests that the texts, in and of themselves, are not perpetuating the dominant culture's AIDS agenda. But the problems with their performances are linked to issues that are not text-specific. While, as I have argued, both performers do challenge the misconceptions about AIDS, it is difficult to separate the form of the performance from its content. In other words, it is hard to view the performance's content outside of its context.

Another difference involves the amount and content of critical responses to their works. First, the NEA controversy has been a topic in all the pieces that have been written about Finley. While the controversy is mentioned in many of the texts on Miller, it is not as prominent an issue. Second, substantially fewer articles have been written on Miller than on Finley. In fact, except for three articles, all the information I acquired on his work was acquired directly from him. For Finley, on the other hand, I was able to locate almost twice as many articles outside the information I obtained through Michael Overn. While both of them have received quite a bit of attention as a result of the controversy, Finley has received more attention than Miller.

Both of these differences lead me to suspect that the content of Miller's performances has determined the amount of press he has received. Because he is dealing with homosexuality and AIDS, something viewed as relatively unimportant to the "general population" (especially when these issues are combined), he has received less attention. The fact that Finley has received more attention suggests that her heterosexuality affords her work more importance and credibility than Miller's, although her work is probably less acceptable than it would be if she were a heterosexual male. A woman's performance appears to be more worthy of publicity than that of a male homosexual.

And because her work addresses significantly more issues, she is assumed to draw more of an audience than Miller. Of the four artists denied grant in 1990, Finley is the only heterosexual. Hence, it could be argued that her plight is more sympathetic to most people than that of Fleck, Hughes, and Miller. Of course, another reason her performances have received more attention is due to the techniques she uses. In comparison to those used by Miller, her performances, particularly her images, are far more spectacular and outrageous.

But a more important issue to be raised involves how this publicity affects the way these performances are read. Although we are accustomed to thinking that the amount of publicity reflects the importance of the project, I believe that in Finley's case her increased publicity is not only detrimental to the public persona she attempts to create, but also to the effectiveness of her work. I begin by returning to the issue of the male gaze.

While many reviewers argue that Finley's performance subverts the male gaze, I would suggest the fact that she is nude raises two important issues. First, because it is discussed in every review, her nudity reflects the male gaze that is inherent in the male-dominated mass media. Additionally, Finley's nudity makes her performance attractive to many men. As Jeanie Forte notes:

> [I]n Finley's case, being catapulted into a higher degree of visibility
> hastened her assimilation into a more commercial audience. In
> venues other than New York, beer-drinking fraternity boys came to
> see the naked woman shove yams up her ass and throw obscenities
> at the crowd.

Forte's quote suggests that Finley's commercialization has led to audiences who are sometimes more interested in her images than the content of her work. Forte concludes, "The threat and power of assimilation is constant, and most visible in the make-up of the performer's audience."[104] Therefore, I believe that the commercialization of Finley's work, resulting from her increased publicity since the NEA controversy, significantly limits its resignifying and subversive power.

These insights regarding Finley's popularity place Miller's lack of attention in a new light. While it could be argued that his invisibility to the media makes his performance ineffective, this invisibility also prevents his work from being misinterpreted, misrepresented, and, more importantly, commercialized. Possibly Miller's text works in the cracks of the media and art institution. Because it is not widely covered, it speaks to a specific audience and serves a consciousness-raising function, similar to feminist theater, that is capable of promoting political action.

Finally, I want to raise some issues regarding how the context of the theater affects the resignifying power of these performances. My first point is that the audiences of these performances are often the "converted," as in the case of the plays discussed in the previous chapter. And, as I have attempted to show in this chapter, the "unconverted" may attend these performances, to put it bluntly, to get a "cheap thrill," as in the case of Finley. Second, the performances are most often presented in small spaces, limiting the number of people who can view their work even more so than the plays discussed in the previous chapter.[105] However, as I suggested, for Miller, these small, informed audiences may eventually engage in political action. Third, because most of the performances occur within spaces designated as theaters they must contend with particular theater conventions, the particular reading formation that audiences often bring to theater events. For example, although these performers address the audience, using the commonplace technique of breaking down the "fourth wall," they are still working within the theatrical frame. Hence, the problems with the apparatus mentioned in chapter 1 are applicable here as well. These performances can potentially fall into the same trap as those of Brecht and artists of the avant-garde tradition.

Similarities exist between performance art and theater, especially when performance art occurs in a space designated as a theater. And changes in the formal elements of the performance (breaking down the fourth wall, using a quasi-autobiographical style, etc.) fail to challenge this reading formation when the performance occurs in a traditional performance space. Even the critics who are supposedly more knowledgeable about this particular form fall back on what they know, reading and interpreting the performance as if it were "theater."

Finley seems to realize, on some level, that her relationship with the theater (and the relationship between performance art and theater) is somewhat problematic. In her interview with Fuoss, Finley laments the fact that many, particularly people in performance studies, use a theatrical frame in order to understand her work. She states, "[T]he fact that I've appropriated the stage setting and people sit down and there's an audience allows theater people to write about my work."[106] Here again she proves my point that audiences often read her performances through a theatrical frame.

In his review, Feingold states that the way Finley delivers her text, which he labels "a kind of spoken musical score," makes it difficult for people who are attempting to "approach her from a theatrical standpoint."[107] However, because she performs in a theater such a perspective is the easiest way to approach her work, especially if someone has no background in performance art. This is a point Feingold fails to address. Indeed, reading the performance through a theatrical frame leads some critics to devalue her incantatory performance style as simply "bad acting."

Additional support for my argument that her work is read as theater is found when we look at the reviews that attempt to explain performance art by comparing it to theater, failing to note its relationship to the visual arts. Finley herself states that she does not see herself "as coming from the theatre world." She goes on to say that "most real performance artists come from more of a visual background rather than from a theatrical setting" and that the visual elements lacking in stand-up comedy and monologues, at least for her, do not constitute performance art.[108]

Because Miller and Finley are both performing in a space designated as a theater, it becomes difficult to challenge the particular reading positions that are associated with mainstream theater. As I suggested, these performances face some of the same problems as the plays discussed in the previous chapter. And, as Spillane has argued, when artists receive public funding, regardless of the content of their work, they are participating in the system that oppresses those whose situations they wish to change.

The attention performance art has received since the controversy has led to larger audiences for these events. Some people who had never witnessed performance art or had no interest in this particular form were led to take an interest in it solely due to the controversy, as in the case of Michael Feingold and Laura Jacobs (two of the critics previously mentioned). As Miller explains, "Performance art is getting new credibility. . . . If nothing else, a year and a half of front-page art stories made it visible."[109] While it could be argued that increased visibility enhances the potential for social change because there are more people witnessing the works, the impact of publicity on Finley's performances suggests otherwise.

In the next chapter I focus on performances that are not read as theater in the traditional sense. These performances avoid many of the problems facing mainstream theater because they occur outside the traditional performance space. Additionally, some of these performances do not allow people the freedom of choice to participate in them. They often occur unexpectedly. Finally, these performances do not require any financial commitment on the part of those who witness/take part in the performance. For these reasons, and others to be discussed, these performances may solve some of the problems affecting both plays and performance art.

NOTES

1. Miller, *Stretch Marks* 165. The ellipses in this quote are part of the original text.

2. Finley, "Our Beating Hearts" 21.

3. Performance art in the United States was heavily influenced by the work of Robert Rauschenberg, John Cage, Merce Cunningham, Allan Kaprow, and others. The books by Sayre and Goldberg both provide additional information on these people, as well as others, who had a strong impact on performance art in the United States prior to 1970.

4. Sayre xiv.

5. Sayre 13.

6. Sayre 14.

7. Sayre 15.

8. Goldberg 8.

9. Heuvel 11.

10. Marranca 137.

11. Sayre 6.

12. Goldberg 9.

13. Glueck H1.

14. Ctd. in Glueck H1.

15. Qtd. in Phelan 134.

16. Andrews 6B.

17. Span and Hall 16.

18. Coffey 90.

19. For discussion of the issues surrounding the controversy over federal funding of the arts see articles by Acker, Glueck, Hughes, Phelan, and Schechner ("Political Realities").

20. T. Walsh 6.

21. Mesce 2A. Frohnmayer was fired shortly after the 1990 controversy.

22. D. Zimmerman 1A.

23. Unless otherwise noted, information on Finley was taken from Linn.

24. Hanson 24; ellipses in original.

25. De Vries F8.
26. Clements 7.
27. Finley, Interview with Richard Schechner 158.
28. Linn C5.
29. Linn C11.
30. Linn C12.
31. Coffey 90.
32. De Vries F9.
33. Evans and Novak A27.
34. Span and Hall 17.
35. Finley, Interview with Kirk Fuoss 1.
36. Haden-Guest 209.
37. De Vries F6.
38. De Vries F6.
39. Span and Hall 17; brackets in original.
40. Finley, *We Keep Our Victims Ready* 124.
41. Finley, Interview with Fuoss 4.
42. Finley, Interview with Fuoss 5.
43. Finley, Interview with Fuoss 4.
44. Finley, Interview with Schechner 154.
45. Finley, Interview with Fuoss 5.
46. L. Shapiro 61.
47. Finley, Interview with Schechner 154.
48. Finley, Interview with Fuoss 6.
49. See, e.g., Case, Dolan.
50. Schuler 132-33.
51. Finley, Letter 10. Subsequent letters to the editor also objected to Schuler's article (see M. Joseph, Moore).
52. Finley, Interview with Fuoss 2.
53. Phelan 134.
54. Nadotti 114
55. For a more detailed explanation of this phrase see both Mulvey and Dolan.
56. Such a reading of this image does not result from Finley's intentions, but how the audience interprets the image. I discuss this issue in more detail in the conclusion to this chapter.

57. Every one of Finley's performances is somewhat different. Although she performs from a pre-written text, she sometimes adds to the script. One example of her adlibing occurred soon after the NEA controversy. Larson explains, after she finished covering her body, she "spread her arms and said, to wild applause, 'This is what they're scared of'" (48).

58. Green D14.

59. Larson 48.

60. Sante 34.

61. Feingold, "Anger" 105. All future references to Feingold in this chapter are to "Anger Unbound."

62. Feingold 108.

63. The three negative reviews are by Kalb, Jacobs, and Spillane.

64. Kalb 112.

65. Sante 36.

66. Sante 37.

67. Sante 37.

68. Sante 37.

69. I am unsure what Sante means by the term duplicating. If he means that no one else can create the same kind of texts, the statement can be viewed as a compliment. In the same vein, if he means no one could perform the texts as she does, it can also be viewed as complimentary, for such is the nature of performance art. As an aside, Finley states in her interview with Fuoss that she does not want others performing her texts, except for her plays, even though some of her performance art texts have been published. She claims the "whole idea of performance work" is that "you're supposed to be creating your own stuff" (8).

70. Faust 120.

71. Jacobs 23.

72. Jacobs 23.

73. Spillane 738.

74. Spillane 738.

75. Unless otherwise noted, the information on Miller was derived from Breslauer.

76. Breslauer 108.

77. Salisbury 5D.

78. The information about his "performance art sermons" was taken from Miller's biography sheet which he sent me (along with numerous articles on his performances) in the fall of 1991. I am indebted to him for this information.

79. Breslauer A3.

80. Breslauer A6.

81. Breslauer A6.

82. Keating, n. pag.

83. Portions of *Stretch Marks* are been included in *Sex/Love/Stories*, a text that has not been published. The latter is a collection of pieces from three of Miller's previous works.

84. Keating, n. pag.

85. Jowitt 114.

86. Mygatt 28A.

87. Linn C11. In responding to a question posed during her interview with Fuoss, Finley refuses to make such a political statement regarding the function of art, although here she is not specifically referring to her work but to art in general. She states, "I don't think that there is necessarily a responsibility for the artist. I think that's something they've placed on things. . . . I think that art is supposed to just be art. I don't see it as a responsibility" (4).

88. Breslauer A5-6.

89. Brandes. The page number for this citation was unobtainable. This article was included in the packet of information Miller sent me, and I was unable to locate the article.

90. Linn C14.

91. Finley, Interview with Fuoss 5.

92. Linn C12.

93. For a more general discussion of the function of the second person in narrative, see HopKins and Perkins, and Capecci.

94. Finley, *We Keep Our Victims Ready* 107.

95. Miller 162.

96. Burnham 11.

97. Burnham 11.

98. Mygatt 38.

99. Miller 166.

100. Finley, *We Keep Our Victims Ready* 123.

101. Finley, *We Keep Our Victims Ready* 125.

102. Finley, *We Keep Our Victims Ready* 124.

103. Finley, *We Keep Our Victims Ready* 143.

104. Forte 268.

105. Not all performance art works are performed in such performance spaces. Some, for example, take place in art galleries; others occur in the street. Thus, the size of the audience for street performances is larger than the two performances I discuss in this chapter.

106. Finley, Interview with Fuoss 3.

107. Feingold 105.

108. Finley, Interview with Fuoss 3.

109. Ctd. in Breslauer A7.

IV

Beyond the Theater:

The AIDS Memorial Quilt, "Condom Day,"

and "Stop the Church"

The two most famous quotes in activist folklore are Joe Hill's
"Don't mourn, organize," and *Mother Jones*'s "Pray for the dead,
but fight like hell for the living."[1]

In this chapter I focus on three performances. The first
performance, displays of the AIDS Memorial Quilt, is sponsored by The
NAMES Project Foundation. Unlike the other performances discussed
in this chapter, this performance is not a "one time only" event. The
Quilt has been displayed almost continuously over the last few years.
The other two performances are demonstrations by ACT UP (AIDS
Coalition to Unleash Power). The first demonstration, "Condom Day,"
occurred in May of 1988. The second, "Stop the Church," occurred in
December of 1989.[2]

In order to discuss the efficacy of these performances for social
change, I first present the history and the goals of the groups sponsoring
these performances. Second, I present a detailed description of each
performance and a comparison between them. Third, I discuss the
responses to these performances as they appeared in various media.
Finally, I analyze the potential of each of these demonstrations for
social change.

HISTORY OF THE NAMES PROJECT

AND ACT UP

The NAMES Project

The NAMES Project Foundation was the result of an idea by Cleve Jones, an Gay/AIDS activist in San Francisco.[3] In November of 1985, Jones attended a candlelight march in memory of Harvey Milk and Mayor George Moscone.[4] As the participants passed by the old Federal Building, they placed placards on the walls of the building in memory of those who had died of AIDS. After seeing the wall, which reminded him of a quilt, he decided that a memorial needed to be created: "There it was, the perfect image—before it was too horrible and too easy to dismiss. I knew that if we could touch hearts with this simple symbol then maybe we could get people to respond."[5]

But it was not until February of 1987 that Jones actually made a panel. In order to help him deal with the loss of a close friend, Jones took a white sheet, spray paint, and stencils, and created what became the first panel for the quilt. His own experience in creating the panel was so powerful that he decided to start The NAMES Project Foundation, the sponsor of the AIDS Memorial Quilt.

Months later, Jones and a friend (Mike Smith) began organizing sewing bees in apartments around San Francisco. And on June 28, 1987, at the San Francisco Lesbian and Gay Freedom Day Parade, forty panels were hung at City Hall from the mayor's balcony. Jones and Smith informed AIDS organizations throughout the country about the project and began to make plans to display the Quilt in October during the National March for Lesbian and Gay Rights in Washington, D.C.

In July, as a number of panels began to arrive from around the country, the group found a place to house the project. A couple of weeks later, sewing machines were donated and a number of people volunteered to sew the individual panels into sections. Three thousand panels arrived at the project prior to the march. But lack of time allowed only 1,920 to make it to Washington.

According to Ruskin, "The NAMES Project is a national effort to create a hand-sewn tribute to the tens of thousands of Americans stricken down by AIDS."[6] Each panel of the Quilt is three by six feet (the size of a grave). Panels can be sewn or painted, and can include any objects (e.g., photos, clothing, letters) that will not damage the fabric. Creators of panels are asked to include a picture of the person they are memorializing and a letter telling about him or her for the project's archives. After they arrive at the NAMES Project, the panels are sewn into blocks of eight. Each block includes panels from one of eight geographic regions so that displays in specific regions include panels made by persons within the region. Panels for the Quilt come from all 50 states as well as a number of foreign countries.

A pamphlet produced by the NAMES Project Foundation states that the NAMES Project's mission is to "illustrate the enormity of the AIDS epidemic by showing the humanity behind the statistics through the AIDS Memorial Quilt." To achieve its mission, the organization established the following goals:

- Increase public awareness of the AIDS epidemic and HIV prevention.

- Offer a creative form of expression for all whose lives have been affected by HIV and AIDS and to preserve the memory of those who have died as a result of the disease.

- Encourage support and the raising of funds for people living with HIV and AIDS and their loved ones.

In an attempt to achieve these goals, the foundation sponsors displays of the Quilt throughout the world.

Three additional goals, although not specifically stated above, include education, unity, and action.[7] One approach to accomplishing the educational goal is to encourage businesses and corporations to sponsor displays of the Quilt for persons who otherwise may not see it (e.g., high school students, racial minorities). Secondly, the project attempts to build unified support in the fight against AIDS. Discussing a 1990 display of the Quilt entitled "Common Threads: An Uncommon

Response," David Lemos, executive director of the project explains that the Quilt is a

> symbol of the "common threads" that bind us in the fight against
> AIDS and strengthen us against the parallel epidemics of ignorance
> and hopelessness. The Quilt is also an example of the "uncommon
> response" of people across America to the uncommon challenges
> of AIDS.[8]

A final goal of the NAMES Project is political action. Outside of raising funds for organizations that provide services for PWAs, which are types of political action, the NAMES Project also attempts to get people to engage in more direct political action. For example, during the "Common Threads" tour, visitors were asked to complete an "Uncommon Response Card" addressed to President Bush. On the card, individuals pledged their commitment in the fight against AIDS by doing volunteer work, providing support for AIDS activities in their communities, and agreeing to speak out against the myths and misinformation surrounding AIDS. On December 1, 1990 (World AIDS Day), the cards were delivered to Bush, and he was asked to increase his commitment in the fight against AIDS.

ACT UP

ACT UP officially began in March of 1987, when Larry Kramer, author of *The Normal Heart* and founder of the Gay Men's Health Crisis (GMHC), gave a speech to members of the New York Lesbian and Gay Community Center. Disheartened by the response of the GMHC to the AIDS epidemic, Kramer asked "Do we want to start a new organization devoted solely to political action?"[9] As a result of the positive response to his question, ACT UP was formed.

ACT UP defines itself as "a diverse, nonpartisan group united in anger and committed to direct action to end the AIDS crisis."[10] Since its inception, chapters have been formed in a number of cities across the country and throughout the world. According to Crimp and Rolston, the group's initial goal was to make drugs available for those infected with HIV/AIDS.[11] Later, the focus of their actions expanded to include issues of funding, education, civil rights, and leadership. For example, from April 29 through May 7, 1988, ACT NOW (a national organization of AIDS activists) organized "Nine Days of Protest." The New York chapter of ACT-UP focused its demonstrations on "homophobia, people with AIDS, people of color, substance abuse, prisons, women, the worldwide crisis, and testing and treatment."[12]

The means adopted by the group to achieve its goals differ from most other organizations. First, the group's structure is non-hierarchical: all the members are volunteers; the few moderators of the meetings give up their posts every six months; decisions are made by group consensus. Second, the group is comprised of a variety of people from different backgrounds, although the majority of its membership consists of young, gay men. Third, the texts produced by ACT UP (including their demonstrations and their graphics) reflect current trends in postmodern theory both in their creation and intent: the authorship for all projects is collective; they claim no originality in regards to the texts they produce (i.e., they admit to "stealing" ideas from various artists, popular advertisements, and other social movements—and encourage others to "steal" their texts); their texts are politically charged. Crimp and Rolston explain, "We don't claim invention of the style or the techniques. We have no patent on the politics or the designs."[13] More specifically, in regards to the graphics, which are often essential elements of ACT UP's demonstrations, Crimp and Rolston state, "The aesthetic values of the traditional art world are of little consequence to AIDS activists. What counts in activist art is its propaganda effect; stealing the procedures of other artists is part of the plan—if it works, we use it."[14] And these graphics are often used to challenge various dominant constructions of AIDS. The final unique quality of ACT UP is that the texts they produce and the actions in which they engage are often quite radical and controversial. As Baker explains, ACT UP's politics are founded on "camp transvestite humor," which intentionally offends and upsets many people in the mainstream "but certainly don't go unnoticed."[15] ACT UP's non-traditional activism lends itself to responses that are not always positive.

THE PERFORMANCES

The AIDS Memorial Quilt

Rather than focusing on a particular display of the Quilt, I have chosen to discuss a typical display as it might occur regardless of location. This decision was made for two reasons. First, displays of the Quilt, despite where they are held, proceed in the same general fashion, especially during the national tours. Second, the small amount of media coverage the Quilt receives in each city would limit my discussion of responses presented in the following section.[16] I begin by discussing the preparation for the display, the opening and closing ceremonies, and other elements that make up the performance.

As David Ford explains, the entire tour is "rigorously organized."[17] Prior to its arrival in a city, a representative from the project assists the local committee with the final arrangements. But even before the representative arrives, the local committee, comprised of volunteers, has chosen the location for the display, arranged media coverage, made hotel accommodations, and has organized fund-raisers and quilting bees within the community. Immediately prior to its unveiling, volunteers and staff spend approximately eight hours setting up the canvas that surrounds each of the 12-by-12 blocks (which serve as a walkway around and between the individual blocks) and placing the folded blocks of panels within the 12-by-12 areas.

During the unveiling ceremony, eight volunteers, wearing white, unfold the blocks of the Quilt individually and attach them to the canvas that surrounds each block. The process, although not perfectly choreographed, is reminiscent of a ritual. Four people enter the center and unfold one part of block. Then the other four do the same. The process continues until the entire block is unfolded. The eight people working with the block lift it up and turn it so that it fits within the surrounding square. Simultaneously, people from the community read the names of the people represented by the panels on display. The readers are encouraged to add to their lists, if they choose to do so, the names of others who have died.

The Quilt stays in a city for no more than three days. There is no admission charge. People are free to come and go as they please. Professionally trained grief counselors are also present to help people in need of support while viewing the Quilt. Additionally, many groups set up tables in the area surrounding the display to collect donations and provide information about AIDS and/or the Quilt. Finally, the displays include a blank panel where visitors can sign their names and/or write a message.

The closure of the display includes a ceremony during which new panels made in the area are added to the Quilt. After the ceremony, volunteers prepare the Quilt for its next stop. Some cities sponsor additional events in conjunction with the Quilt's visit. For example a display in Washington included a meeting of AIDS activists and an interfaith memorial service. The closing ceremony occurred at the Kennedy Center for the Performing Arts during which letters written by those who had sent in quilts were read, interspersed with music and dancing. Some cities have also included candlelight vigil marches as a part of the Quilt's visit.

Before moving on to ACT UP's demonstrations, I want to discuss a tour that began in February of 1992 and ended in June. The tour was entitled *An Event in Three Acts: The National Tour*. Act One was the second national tour of *Heart Strings* (a musical revue), which coincides with the displays of the Quilt.[18] *Heart Strings* was first produced in 1985 in Atlanta in order to benefit DIFFA (Design Industries Foundation for AIDS).[19] Each year since its inception the performance has changed. According to David Sheppard, the executive producer of the production, this year's production

> celebrates the thousands of volunteers, the organizations and the heroes that have made an immeasurable difference in the lives of people living with AIDS and the loved ones surrounding them.
>
> We sing and dance about the fundraisers and partygivers with style and flair. We acknowledge the caregivers with touching ballads and talk about sex in the 90's [sic] with humor and cutting edge choreography. We remember those lost and bring a light of hope to those living with AIDS. And in the grand finale, we ask each of you to join in our crusade.[20]

Act Two was the actual display of the AIDS Memorial Quilt in various cities throughout the United States. Act Three was entitled "The Next Step." According to the pamphlet for the tour, "Many people feel inspired to action after viewing the Quilt or seeing *Heart Strings*. This is 'Act Three' of *An Event in Three Acts*: getting involved in the fight against HIV/AIDS in your community." The pamphlet provides numerous examples of how individuals can become actively involved. Some examples include making a panel for the Quilt, learning about AIDS and HIV transmission and educating others, volunteering time at an AIDS/HIV service organization, writing letters to elected officials, and/or donating food or money to AIDS/HIV organizations.

The largest and most publicized display of the Quilt occurred in October 1992 when the entire Quilt was displayed in Washington, D.C. The sheer magnitude of this display and the people who came to show their support made it difficult to ignore. When it was finally unfurled, it included 20,064 panels and covered approximately 15 acres. (The opening ceremony had to be delayed due to bad weather.) It is estimated that 300,000 people saw the Quilt during the 1992 Washington Display.[21]

As of February 1995, the panel included 28,972 panels, which, unfortunately, represent only 12 percent of AIDS-related deaths in the United States. The NAMES Project Foundation, according to Cleve Jones, is "the largest AIDS organization in the country in terms of grassroots participation" although it does not have the largest budget or staff. The panels alone weigh 34 tons and are the size of 17 football fields without the walkways. When the walkways are added, the numbers become 39 and 19, respectively. In addition to panels representing people from all 50 states and Puerto Rico, 29 countries worldwide have contributed panels as well.[22]

"Condom Day"

"Condom Day" occurred during "Spring AIDS Action '88," which took place from April 29 through May 7, 1988.[23] Throughout the country, AIDS activist groups associated with ACT NOW (AIDS

Coalition to Network, Organize and Win) engaged in protests for nine days, dealing with a variety of issues related to the AIDS crisis.

In New York, May 4, 1988, was designated "Women's Day," and that night ACT UP's Women's Committee demonstrated at Shea Stadium. The purpose of this demonstration was to get straight men to take responsibility for their partners' health because, as Crimp and Rolston note, "official advice about safe sex practices is almost always directed at *women*."[24] In the AIDS epidemic, birth control pills, diaphragms, and other means through which *women* can prevent pregnancy are no longer an issue. Condoms or abstinence are the only means to prevent a woman from contracting AIDS, and the message of these activists was that *men* need to take responsibility for protecting their sexual partners. For this reason, the demonstration was appropriately called "Condom Day" by the activists.

During the baseball game the activists gave out pamphlets and condoms, held up banners, shouted slogans, and, because they had purchased three blocks of seats (they bought 400 tickets), they were allowed to flash their messages about safe sex on the stadium's electronic billboard. A pamphlet that was given to those attending the game was entitled "AIDS is No Ball Game," and it appropriately used the language of a baseball game as a metaphor for their message:

> SINGLE: Only *one* woman has been included in government-sponsored tests for new drugs for AIDS;
>
> DOUBLE: Women diagnosed with AIDS die *twice* as fast as men;
>
> TRIPLE: The number of women with AIDS has *tripled* since the 1984 World Series;
>
> THE GRAND SLAM: Most men *still* don't use condoms.[25]

The slogans that were included on their banners and in their chants also metaphorically reappropriated the language of the game: "No Glove No Love," "Don't Balk at Safer Sex," "Strike Out AIDS."

"Stop the Church"

The final performance, "Stop the Church," is perhaps ACT UP's most well known demonstration.[26] On December 10, 1989, ACT UP and WHAM! (Women's Health Action and Mobilization) went to St. Patrick's Cathedral in New York City. The goal of the demonstration was to challenge Cardinal O'Connor's position on abortion, safe sex education, and the use of condoms. The protest was publicized all over the city, and, as a result, the police and church officials were aware of the protest, including the fact that some of the activists planned to demonstrate inside the church during Mass. Cardinal O'Connor and the police were prepared.[27]

The protest began outside the church at 9:30, where more than 4,500 people had gathered. Police officers had set up barricades to prevent the protesters from interfering directly with those who wanted to enter. Crimp and Rolston describe the area inside the barricades as being so cramped that it appeared as if this condition was created intentionally by the police, many of whom were Catholic, to encourage a violent response and make the demonstrators appear angry and out of control. Crimp and Rolston also claim that outside the barricades one protestor was violently attacked by a number of these "good Christian cops."[28]

The protestors held up signs that read "Stop This Man" (with a picture of Cardinal O'Connor), "Curb Your Dogma," and "Danger—Narrow-Minded Church Ahead." They shouted the "Seven Deadly Sins of Cardinal O'Connor and the Church Politicians," each of which reflected how O'Connor and other church officials were guilty through their negligence/ignorance of women, lesbians, gay men, drug users, and others. By comparison, what occurred on the streets was relatively calm, although 68 protesters were arrested.

Inside St. Patrick's, as Cardinal O'Connor began his mass, activists came out of their seats and staged a "die-in" in the aisle of the church. ("Die-ins" are often used by ACT UP to show how the negligence of their given target affects PWAs.) Some threw condoms and attached themselves to pews. One protestor loudly blew a whistle and screamed "You're murdering us. Stop killing us." Others joined in with the vocal protests until the music began to play and the parishioners began singing, drowning out the voices of the protesters. During communion, Tom Keane (who used to be an altar boy) grabbed a communion wafer (which Catholics view as the body of Christ) and dropped it on the floor. Shortly thereafter, the police entered and began to remove the "dead" on stretchers. "We're fighting for your lives, too," screamed the last of the protestors being carried away. As the police exited the church, O'Connor stated, "We must never respond to hatred with hatred, but only with love, compassion, and understanding. Mass has ended, go in peace."[29] Forty-three activists from inside the church were arrested, bringing the total number of arrests to 111.

RESPONSES TO EVENTS

The differences between these performances are highlighted when we look at the amount and type of press that each demonstration received, as well as how they dealt with the AIDS issue. In this section, I discuss the responses to each of these events individually by summarizing the comments that were made about them in various printed media. This summary is followed by a brief comparison of the responses to each performances.

The AIDS Memorial Quilt

In his article "How to Have Promiscuity in an Epidemic," Crimp briefly mentions the Quilt in the context of the 1987 gay and lesbian rights march in Washington. More importantly, however, he describes the "right wing" response to its unveiling. Crimp explains that in November of 1987, *Campus Review* included an article by Gary Bauer, who was an assistant to Reagan and the Administration's AIDS policy spokesperson.[30] The article, "AIDS and the College Student," appeared on the front page of the paper with a political cartoon entitled "The AIDS Quilt." The picture includes two males who are sewing panels for a quilt. The first panel, which is being sewn by a homosexual, says "sodomy." The second panel, sewn by a drug user, says "IV Drugs."[31] In the article, which surrounds the cartoon, Bauer argues:

> Many of today's education efforts are what could be called
> "sexually egalitarian." That is, they refuse to distinguish or even
> appear to prefer one type of sexual practice over another. Yet
> medical research shows that sodomy is probably the most efficient
> method to transfer the AIDS virus [sic] as well as other
> diseases—for obvious reasons.[32]

Taken together, the article and the cartoon serve to perpetuate the idea that AIDS is a gay disease and an affliction of IV drug users. Furthermore, the Quilt, according to the cartoon, signifies IV drug use and sodomy. The cartoonist seems to suggest that the Quilt approves (perhaps celebrates) these behaviors—behaviors which Bauer and other conservatives view as morally wrong.

Of all the responses to the Quilt, none is as hostile as the aforementioned cartoon. However, the small amount of information about the Quilt, in both mainstream magazines and scholarly journals, suggests a hesitancy on the part of writers to deal with the Quilt. One reason for this limited response, particularly scholarly or academic works, may be due to the uniqueness of this particular event. That is, it could be argued that unlike more traditional forms of protest, e.g., demonstrations, less common forms of protest need more time to be incorporated into theories of culture, rhetoric, and performance.

Similarly, a second explanation for this hesitancy may be a result of writers not knowing *how* to deal with it. Should it be viewed as a work of art or as a political statement? Traditional notions of what is art (or, more importantly, what a quilt is) would deny the politics attached to the AIDS Quilt. However, such denial, given the connotations attached to AIDS, is impossible. Rob Baker, in his text on artistic works about AIDS provides some support for these explanations. He asserts, the Quilt "has been analyzed as art, theater, politics, spirituality and even (in a panel at the 1993 Modern Language Association convention) as "rhetoric."[33]

One conflict over what the Quilt is and is not can be found in an article by Enid Zimmerman and a response to the article, written by Gilbert Clark. The primary issue Zimmerman confronts is how to address multiculturalism and art education. One approach that has received little attention, she argues, is a multicultural and social reconstructionist approach. This approach "stresses a social action position in which racism, sexism, and inequity are discussed and attended to as much as the cultural dimension of education." The reason this approach has received so little attention, she claims, is because it forces teachers to deal with "sensitive issues."[34] And Zimmerman uses the NAMES Project as an example of one work of art that can help teachers address these important, but sensitive, issues.

Clark, on the other hand, takes issue with Zimmerman's proposal. Essentially, what Clark objects to is the mixing of art and politics. His view is that "Art is neither political science nor social studies."[35] Regarding the Quilt, Clark argues:

> there are more accessible and easier to use images that do not connote the public health threat-AIDS-sexual transmission-homosexuality-epidemic issues that the NAMES project would cause teachers to confront. I am not suggesting that these are taboo topics, but that they are not critical to understanding celebrations, quilting, or group-project art works, nor are they critical content for an ART class at any grade level.[36]

Thus, for Clark, art and politics should not be mixed in an art class. For him, politics is neither the purpose of art education, nor is it important for understanding a work of art. Although Clark and Zimmerman are talking specifically about art education, they also provide an explanation for the hesitancy on the part of many writers to deal with the Quilt. As Clark suggests, dealing with art objects like the Quilt is just too difficult.

Clark also reveals a second, more specific, reason for this hesitancy: the link between the Quilt and the connotations of AIDS. Because many of the means of transmission are considered to be unacceptable types of behavior, especially by the dominant culture, writers, especially those in mainstream presses, may find it difficult to talk about the Quilt. The issue facing these writers, it seems to me, is how to talk about the Quilt without appearing to condone the behaviors that lead to its transmission. The difficulty in accomplishing this task may explain the response to the Quilt in magazines such as *Time*,

Newsweek, and *U.S. News and World Report*, all of which have paid little attention to the Quilt. And when they do report on it, the amount of space devoted to it is minimal.

Time devotes less than a column to the 1988 display of the Quilt in Washington, focusing mainly on a few trivial facts about it. Although the article begins by describing the Quilt as "one of the nation's most moving memorials," it ends shortly thereafter by telling us that "While the quilt is on display outdoors, it will be guarded by 300 volunteers, who have been trained to fold it in as little as 45 seconds should the weather turn foul."[37] Could the writer not think of anything more important to say about this "moving memorial" than the fact that if it rains it only takes 45 seconds to fold something the size of eight football fields?

Additionally, the article mentions nothing about the people who are represented by the Quilt. Instead, it suggests a link between the Quilt and gays and lesbians by stating that its "unveiling will culminate a week-long series of events celebrating the anniversary of last year's March on Washington by gays and lesbians."[38] Other articles dealing with same display, regardless of their context, make no connection between the gay and lesbian march and the display of the Quilt. The decision to mention the march and to place the Quilt in the context of its anniversary serves to marginalize the Quilt, to distance it from mainstream culture by implying that it is connected to the gay and lesbian movement.

The article on the Quilt in *U.S. News and World Report*, "The Best of America: The Culture," is also brief. On the first page there is a picture of the Quilt in front of the U.S. Capitol and literally thousands of visitors. On the right hand side, overlapping the picture, we are told that according to a poll they conducted, the Quilt was voted the "work of art with the greatest social impact" by "artists, writers and curators." But while the brief paragraph on the next page discusses the quilting tradition and talks about how the Quilt gives voice to those silenced by the epidemic, the most vivid (and disturbing) information about the Quilt is presented in large letters on the first page above the information about the survey: "When the cultural history of the 1980s is written, one event will overshadow all others. For painters, playwrights and dancers,

AIDS has been a cataclysm, felling thousands and echoing through many living artists' work."[39]

The problem with this statement is that it places the value of these artists' lives over others who have died. No mention is made of people outside the arts, people who are less visible, who have died of AIDS. Similar to Feingold's argument (discussed in chapter 2) about the effect of the AIDS epidemic on the artistic community, this statement valorizes the lives of those who are viewed as making an important contribution to "American Culture." Hence, AIDS is signified as an affliction of artists. And given the number of gay artists, AIDS becomes covertly linked with homosexuality. As in the *Time* article, both AIDS and the Quilt are distanced from heterosexuals.

Before discussing the responses to the Quilt in various newspapers, which, like these magazines, are also written for the "general population," I discuss three articles included in magazines that have a more specific audience. The first article, from *Christian Century*, takes a uniquely personal approach to the Quilt. In the article, Jerry Gentry describes his experience with the Quilt on Easter Weekend in 1989 and spends a significant amount of time focusing on the link between AIDS and homosexuals:

> All types of persons are represented on the quilts, but the often discomforting connection between AIDS and homosexuality is prevalent. . . .
> Given the homosexual community's tenuous relationship with mainstream society, the NAMES Project aptly provides freedom to express frustration over a disease that seems to kill selectively, and that often selects the already snubbed.[40]

While these statements reiterate the view of AIDS as a "gay disease," Gentry uses the link to challenge the Christian community, especially Southern Baptists, to acknowledge gay existence. In a rather subtle way, he condemns those within the religious community who ignore the fact that there are gay people who participate in religious services. He states:

> Homosexuality, indelibly stained by secular/cultural prejudice, is not even acknowledged as a cog on a sprocket in the machine. . . .
> Exiled within their own communities, gays continue to play music

and sing and pray and worship and praise God, hoping for the day
when their place in the community is not qualified and silenced by
their nature.[41]

Thus, Gentry uses the Quilt as a way to talk about the relationship
between homosexuals and a religion that oppresses them. But it could
be argued that, in doing so, he further solidifies the link between
homosexuals and AIDS. For only once does he specifically mention a
panel created for someone who is not homosexual.

However, after describing this panel, which was made for a
small child, Gentry challenges the belief held by some that AIDS is a
punishment sent by God: "The message [from this panel] crystallizes
that if God is punishing sinners by giving them AIDS, God wields a
clumsy and blunt ax."[42] It is Gentry's uniquely personal and positive
response to the Quilt, which is placed within a religious context, that
challenges the belief that persons with AIDS are guilty of a sin.
Regardless of how they contracted AIDS, Gentry suggests, perhaps too
subtly, that homosexuality should not be viewed as a sin.

A more objective approach to the Quilt, written by Elinor
Fuchs, was published in *The Nation*. While Fuchs spends some time
describing its history and contents, most of the article is dedicated to
discussing the political nature of the Quilt. The thesis of her argument
is that although the coordinators of the Quilt "claim no political purpose
. . . the quilt is itself politics, a masterpiece of grass-roots community
organizing and a focus for further organizing wherever it appears."[43]
Having viewed the Quilt in Washington, Fuchs compares it to other
nearby memorials. She argues that unlike other Washington memorials,
which are "the deliberative result of official hierarchies," perhaps "the
most moving and at the same time most politically suggestive thing
about the quilt" is its

> lived tackiness, the refusal of so many thousands of quilters to
> solemnize their losses under the aesthetics of mourning. . . . The
> AIDS Quilt project, responding to an unprecedented situation,
> entirely lacks the centralized vision and apparatus of modern public
> mourning.[44]

Fuchs' response to the Quilt is unique in that she stresses the political nature of the Quilt and downplays the cathartic nature of panel making and quilt viewing.[45] In fact, she draws a comparison between the AIDS Quilt and quilting in the nineteenth century, suggesting that quilting was "an implicit model for political organization" as well as "a social activity."[46]

Finally, I want to mention an article that appeared in the *Chronicle of Higher Education* describing the display of the Quilt at Dartmouth College in the Spring of 1991. In this article Lawrence Biemiller is careful to stress the variety of people who attended the display and those represented by the various panels. Like Fuchs, Biemiller takes a more objective approach to the Quilt.

Biemiller attempts to show the strong impact the Quilt had on those who witnessed the display by including comments by those who attended. He takes great care in stressing that AIDS can affect anyone and that people who viewed the Quilt were moved by the experience. The comments include responses from university students, faculty, and community members. In addition, comments from two gay students at the university are included in his article. One said he felt the Quilt provided heterosexual students a safe way to support the gay community. However, another gay student felt that many people view the Quilt as "a gay thing" and, as a result, a number of people, students and non-students, did not go see it.[47] The dominant culture's response to AIDS, its attempt to marginalize it, makes this response an obvious one. If AIDS is a "gay disease," the Quilt, which pays tribute to those who have died of AIDS, must be "a gay thing."

But for those who did attend, according to Biemiller, the display was extremely powerful. The responses to the Quilt as a memorial were all positive and emotional. The AIDS Quilt, he implies, represents a human tragedy, and the emotional response of individuals to the Quilt suggests that those who participated understood that AIDS is not something that affects only certain groups of people, but has the potential to affect everyone.

The articles by Gentry, Fuchs, and Biemiller suggest the powerful impact the Quilt has had on its viewers. But for Biemiller and Gentry, the Quilt produces an emotional outlet. It allows the visitors to experience and express grief over the loss of people they may or may not know. In this sense, the Quilt functions much like any other memorial. For Fuchs, on the other hand, the Quilt is different. It allows those whose voices are usually silenced to be heard. For this reason, the Quilt is different from other memorials. Fuchs does not, like Biemiller, attempt to conceal the differences under the auspices of humanity. Nor does she use the Quilt as a way to get at another issue, as does Gentry. Instead, she suggests that the Quilt is a powerful monument, one that is both political in its intent and able to promote action on the part of those who participate in the experience.[48]

In another article by Fuchs, published in *American Theatre*, Fuchs actually refers to the Quilt as a performance. In her essay "The Performance of Mourning," Fuchs argues that "the Quilt is more relaxed, more inclusive, more sensual, more human, more *theatrical* than anything previously imagined in the protocols of mourning."[49] Fuchs likens the Quilt to a cemetery with "Rows and rows of marble headstones etched with teddy bears, Hawaiian shirts and Mickey Mouse. . . . The Quilt is cemetery as All Fool's Days, a carnival of the sacred, the homely, the joyous and the downright tacky, resisting, even *in extremis*, the solemnity of mourning." Responding to Fuchs, Rob Baker states:

> Fuch's initially surprising analysis of the Quilt as a "performance". . . makes the most sense. . . . However, at the same time that the Quilt is performance or a kind of camp celebration, more like a wake than a visit to the funeral home, it also has a very serious, solemn, and perhaps sacred purpose: to honor in death persons who, more often than not were not accorded proper honor and respect in life, especially during their final disease.[50]

I include Baker's comment because I find his understanding of performance (or perhaps of Fuch's argument) somewhat limited because he appears unable, initially, to accept her argument. When he does, he makes sense of the Quilt as performance from a traditional perspective. In other words, he fails to see that part of the performance includes the "serious, solemn, and . . . sacred purpose"of honoring persons who have died.

The newspaper articles on the Quilt are much longer than those discussed earlier that appear in mainstream magazines. Most of the articles spend a great deal of time describing the Quilt and its history, and include quotes from both visitors and coordinators of the project. Some of the articles are melodramatic in their tone.[51] Others are more factual, similar to Biemiller's article. None, however, are personal. The authors of these articles clearly distance themselves from their subject. But one theme emerges from these articles—at least those that go beyond describing its logistics—is that viewing the Quilt is a moving, emotional experience to which everyone can relate, regardless of whether they know someone who has died. As Ford asserts, "Symbolically, [the Quilt] will bring a 'message of compassion and caring' to those Americans who still view AIDS as a stigmatizing disease."[52] Or, as Donohoe states, "One of the weekend's clear priorities was to personalize AIDS as an 'equal opportunity disease' that is no respecter of lifestyle."[53]

The Quilt is treated as a memorial—an emotional outlet, a place where people can express grief over the loss of those who have died, regardless of whether or not they personally knew someone. Many of the articles discuss how the Quilt attempts to challenge the stereotypes of persons with AIDS. If they mention panels, they generally present a cross section of persons who have died, but often explain how the person contracted AIDS, especially when the person memorialized is a child.

Bronski argues that homosexuals often respond positively to the pity and sentimentality that is often found in "mainstream journalism" about AIDS. However, such a response, he explains, is problematic because it is a type of "false consciousness" in that people who hate homosexuals are probably happy that gays are dying. As a result, these people use the information to blame homosexuals for the spread of AIDS to heterosexuals.[54] What Bronski is saying in regards to mainstream journalism about AIDS is also true, as I have attempted to show, of how the Quilt is represented. In many, but certainly not all cases, the Quilt is equated with homosexuals. As a result, it further marginalizes gay people, often making them scapegoats for AIDS.

In summary, the newspaper articles attempt to create sympathy for all persons who have died, paying little attention to those who are living with AIDS. And AIDS is not, for the most part, signified as a "gay disease." But, as a whole, these are all reports. They explain the history of the Quilt and the responses of those who work with it and have viewed it; however, none of them explores, in any significant detail, the political implications of the Quilt or its ability to get people to commit to any action after viewing the Quilt. Instead, the only action that takes place occurs when one views the Quilt, according to the articles: an expression of sadness and grief over those who have died.[55] The Quilt, according to these articles, is a place where people can go to mourn, not act.

"Condom Day"

While Josh Gamson remarks that the Shea Stadium demonstration received "wide coverage the following day," a review of newspapers and magazines published that week suggests that the coverage he refers to was probably local and most likely found in the visual, rather than print, media.[56] In fact, of the two articles located, neither spends a significant amount of time talking about the demonstration. The first article, included in the *New York Times*, appeared more than two months after the demonstration. The second article, included in *Newsweek*, devotes one paragraph to the demonstration.[57]

Morgan's article is an attempt to explain how ACT UP has changed its tactics. Using "Condom Day" as an example, he states:

> While disruptive, surgically planned demonstrations are still ACT UP's hallmark, the Shea Demonstration took its controversial message out of Manhattan to working-class Queens, marking the group's growing sophistication and its movement toward more mainstream forms of protest.[58]

Perhaps it is only the disruptive tactics that ACT UP had used prior to "Condom Day" that makes Morgan call this demonstration "more mainstream." And in comparison to "Stop the Church," this demonstration appears to be more moderate. However, the message that these protesters delivered was certainly radical, given the dominant construction of AIDS, and the choice to take it to a baseball game, which is linked to some of the most traditional American values, was a very effective choice.

The few articles reporting on this demonstration, especially in comparison to those that talk about "Stop the Church," are relatively gentle. The message of the activists is not misrepresented in these publications, if it is discussed at all. However, Morgan's article is disturbing because it does not really examine the issues that were being raised by the activists. The article's tone is rather condescending—it focuses more on the activists' behaviors than the issues at hand. Morgan seems to be patting the activists on their heads because their behavior conformed to non-disruptive standards that the dominant culture deems appropriate. He seems to be saying that these people have finally learned how to behave. And while he does mention the issues of this protest and others, the title, "Mainstream Strategy for AIDS Group," foregrounds their behavior and places the issues in the background.

Given the minimal response to this demonstration, it is impossible to draw any conclusions about how the demonstration was "read." Thus, a more interesting question is why the demonstration received so little publicity. The lack of response can be attributed to a number of factors. First, in comparison to the Quilt, this event occurred only once and took place in one city.

Similarly, although a large number of people attend baseball games, the demonstration was most likely overshadowed by the game itself. The existing media practices have created standardized methods for wide coverage of the games. But these stories, which include personal information about players and sometimes avid fans, are so entrenched for sportswriters and their readers, that creating a space in traditional sports discourse would be almost impossible. And the large amount of newspaper space devoted to this standardized discourse probably deters other journalists from looking at sports events for other kinds of stories.

Second, the demonstrators were expressing views that many want to ignore. The AIDS issue, in the context of this demonstration, was probably irrelevant to those in attendance. Many heterosexuals do not want to believe that they are at risk for AIDS. Hence, the lack of response to the demonstration may be a method utilized by the press to protect these people. Avoiding the issues of the demonstration allow the mass media to perpetuate the belief that AIDS is not a threat to heterosexual men or women.

Finally, and perhaps most importantly, it was difficult for the mass media to use the event to reaffirm the dominant discourse about AIDS. Support for this assertion is found in a comparison between "Condom Day" and "Stop the Church."

"Stop the Church"

The "Stop the Church" demonstration was used by the national and local media to show how "radical" AIDS activists are in pursuing their goals. The responses to the event foregrounded the issues of religion and backgrounded the AIDS issue. In addition, these responses perpetuated the dominant construction of AIDS—primarily the belief that AIDS is a "gay disease." The mass media presented the demonstrators as sacrilegious because, not only did they enter the church, they desecrated the body of Christ.[59]

Because O'Connor knew that the activists would be entering his church, he had photocopies of his sermon ready. During the singing, the altar boys are seen handing out copies. Also, according to Crimp and Rolston, O'Connor

> filled the church not with the usual Sunday faithful, but with Catholic militants and undercover police. Mayor Koch was also there to side with his old buddy. . . . The heavily reported "outrage" of the parishioners at the disruption of the mass was therefore completely orchestrated.[60]

In other words, ACT UP's performance in St. Patrick's was met with another performance, one that ended up looking like a sacred drama in which "evil" was destroyed (or at least quieted, for the time being) and "good" triumphed. O'Connor beautifully cast his roles and therefore ended up playing the lead—the martyr. And this view was reflected in the media's coverage of the event.

As the activists expected, the end result of the media's coverage was that Cardinal O'Connor became the martyr, and the demonstrators, "heathens." As Crimp and Rolston suggest, "To the press, the politicians, and even to conservative gay 'leaders' STOP THE CHURCH went too far: because we went inside the cathedral, we denied Catholic parishioners their freedom of religion."[61] Thus, the issues of the protest were turned around—freedom to worship became primary and the deadly issue of AIDS, secondary.[62] In a more general sense, the mass media became the means through which the dominant culture's values were affirmed, and the success of the strategies used by those involved in this demonstration became questionable. The media's response to this demonstration suggests that "Stop the Church" was probably the most controversial event in ACT UP's history.

The controversy surrounding this demonstration resurfaced in the fall of 1991 when PBS decided not to air Robert Hilferty's video on the demonstration. According to John Coleman, a vice-president of PBS decided that the video "did not meet PBS standards for broadcast quality and that it was 'inappropriate for airing because its pervasive tone of ridicule overwhelms its critique of policy.'"[63] This decision created a controversy between PBS and "gay groups," as Coleman calls them, that led some local PBS stations to air it. The biggest controversy over airing the video occurred in Los Angeles when Cardinal Roger Mahony, placing an ad in the *Los Angeles Times*, asked people to call KCET (the PBS affiliate in Los Angeles) and express their anger over airing the video.[64] The video was shown, framed by a discussion between two "media experts."

What I find most interesting about this controversy is that it came only a couple of months after a similar conflict surrounding *Tongues Untied*—a documentary about black, gay men by Marlon Riggs. However, while *Point of View* decided that *Stop the Church* should not be aired, local PBS affiliates were allowed to decide whether or not to show *Tongues Untied*. Some decided to air the documentary, although many of them decided to do it late at night. Interestingly, *Tongues Untied* includes nudity, explicit sexual references, and profanity. *Stop the Church* includes no nudity, very little profanity, and no sexual references. The decision not to air the *Stop the Church* video seems to suggest that some taboos are greater than others—that producers and viewers should be given a choice whether or not to watch a film on black homosexuals, but challenges against a religious institution are inappropriate viewing material for anyone, even on a series that is dedicated to showing different "points of view."

A comparison between the amount of attention afforded "Condom Day" and "Stop the Church" supports my earlier assertion that it is hard to create space for non-traditional forms of discourse. Such a comparison also suggests that only the most "radical" demonstrations will be covered in the media. Because "Condom Day" was relatively harmless—even innocuous—the press could not do with it what it later did with "Stop the Church." And although the Quilt, in comparison to "Condom Day," has received significantly more attention in the media, this attention is probably due to the number of times the Quilt has been displayed as well as the ability of the press to focus on an issue that everyone relates to—the expression of grief.

What seems clear in these examples is that in order for these performances to succeed on a large scale they have to control how the media (re)presents both the protest and the issues. If given the opportunity, as they were in the "Stop the Church" demonstration, the media seems predisposed to downplay relevant issues that are of vital importance to the demonstrators and, more significantly, perpetuate misconceptions about AIDS. Members of ACT UP know they must control the media. As one woman states, "We must communicate *through* the media, not *to* the media. Use the media to get our message across to the people whose attention we have grabbed with our event."[65]

In the "Stop the Church" demonstration, however, Cardinal O'Connor seemed to be more effective in "speaking through the media" than was ACT UP. Many activists agree that the attention they received in the media was not good, though it gave them some publicity. As Larry Kramer argued in one ACT UP meeting, "We couldn't have gotten worse publicity than the Church action, and that put us on the map."[66] ACT UP received nationwide coverage as a result of this demonstration. Thus, in the eyes of some, the demonstration was a success.[67] But the kind of attention that ACT UP received after the demonstration, does not necessarily lead to social change.

EFFECTIVENESS

Although the performances discussed in the previous chapters differ in form, there are, as I have suggested, some similarities between the two. First, the performances in the previous chapters occurred in places designated for performances.[68] Hence, although the performers may challenge the conventions of traditional theater performances, they are still confined by the performance space. Distinctions exist between the placement of the performer or performers and the audience. Secondly, the number of persons viewing these performances is limited. The audience size is determined by the number of times the performance is presented, the number of people the space can hold, and the cost of the performance. Finally, the audience members choose to attend the event. They make an active effort to attend the performance.

In contrast, the performances discussed in this chapter did not occur in spaces designated as theaters, and the size of the audience was not so constrained. In fact, the "audiences" for these performances do not view themselves as audiences in the traditional sense. As a result, the people witnessing these performances are not constrained by theater conventions. There is no "stage" and no cost of admission. For these reasons, audiences for these performances are much larger. Additionally, unlike the performances discussed in the previous chapters, the texts of these performances are not developed from a pre-written text. Instead, the texts emerge as the participants engage in the performance. Finally, the issue of choice is defined very differently as a result of where these performances occur. Because they occur in very public spaces, people often do not have the freedom to choose whether or not they wish to witness the event. Of course, the people who do not wish to view the event can choose to leave. And this is true for any performance event, although social rules dictate that one should only leave the theater during intermission. However, for two of the performances discussed in this chapter, the choice to participate in an event as a spectator is not made prior to the beginning of the performance, and the decision not to

participate in the event can be made at any time after the performance
has begun.

These factors could potentially enhance the ability of the
performances discussed in this chapter to promote social change. Such
a comparison helps explain why one of these performances may have
been more successful than another. In order to compare these
performances I focus on three issues: (1) how confrontational the
performances were; (2) who was targeted by the event; and (3) what
codes affected the audience's response to the events. Each of these
issues helps explain the efficacy of these performances for social
change.

First, the differences between these performances suggest some
interesting findings regarding what is acceptable and unacceptable in
society in terms of how confrontational tactics are received. Unlike the
"Stop the Church" demonstration, "Condom Day" and the Quilt were
non-confrontational events. In "Condom Day" the activists did not
interrupt or stop the game in any way, nor did they prevent the fans
from watching the game. No special concessions or security measures
were required to accommodate the demonstrators. The demonstration
became part of the event, as a kind of sideshow. The demonstrators
appear to have thought through every step of the demonstration in order
to make it more acceptable for the fans. For example, they chose their
graphics used to complement their message very carefully. An example
of an image created for the nine days of protest that the activists chose
not to include in this demonstration was a picture of an erect penis. The
title of this poster was "SEXISM REARS ITS UNPROTECTED
HEAD." Below, in smaller letters, was written "Men: Use Condoms or
Beat it." The final message, printed on the bottom of the poster was
"AIDS KILLS WOMEN." While obviously relevant to their message,
the women did not include this very graphic poster during the
demonstration; however, ACT UP members found the phrase "Men: Use
Condoms or Beat it" so appealing that it was printed on t-shirts and
stickers.[69]

The "Stop the Church" demonstration drastically changed, at
least for a short time, the structure of the event in which the
demonstration occurred. The people in the church were directly

confronted by the activists and were unable to continue to worship in the same way during the event. The Quilt was the least confrontational of all because participants had a choice as to whether or not they wished to attend. The event was not staged as an intervention into another event, i.e., a baseball game or a church service. Instead it was an event in and of itself.

Second, the performances differ in regards to their targeted audience and the goals they wished to accomplish. The Quilt did not target a specific group of people. Instead, it attempted to attract all people, regardless of race, religion, gender, economic status, or sexual orientation. Hence, the goals of the Quilt, as I mentioned earlier, were numerous. But in regards to taking action, the planners of the event did not specify any particular course of action. The targeted audience for "Condom Day" was a specific group of people—heterosexual men. Additionally, the goal of the event was also specific—to get heterosexual men to take responsibility for the health of their sexual partners. "Stop the Church" also targeted a specific institution—the Catholic Church. The goal of the demonstration was to prompt people to question the Church's position on contraception and homosexuality. However, Cardinal O'Connor became a more specific target for the demonstration, first because he is the church's representative in New York City and second, because he had been especially vocal on issues related to AIDS (e.g., homosexuality, birth control). Consequently, the demonstrators were perceived as attacking one particular man—a highly respected religious leader, at that.

Finally, one of the most interesting differences between these events is the codes that were used to help these events achieve their goals and what these codes represent or signify. In other words, in the context in which they occurred, each performance attempted to activate certain reading codes or interpretive codes within the audience. Although each of these demonstrations was operating within codes that were familiar to their audiences, the way they reappropriated or resignified what these codes meant had an effect on what the performances could do.

As I suggested earlier, a baseball game is embedded in American culture. It is linked to some of the most traditional American values, and therefore linked to specific codes with which its audience was familiar. Obviously people do not think about, nor do they want to think about, AIDS while watching America's favorite sport. As one fan put it, "AIDS is a fearful topic. This is totally inappropriate."[70] Yes, AIDS is a fearful topic, and this is exactly the point the activists were attempting to make: AIDS can become as much a part of every American's life as a baseball game if people continue to ignore it or think that it cannot happen to them. The activists were mixing something that many would argue is an essential part of American life with the potential for death. In that sense, the baseball game becomes a perfect place to distribute their message. The codes of the baseball game were metaphorically reappropriated into the discourse about AIDS.

A quilt, like a baseball game, is also linked to some of the more traditional American values. Quilting, according to Susan Roach, is a "traditional American folk art form that has been transmitted through American culture for over three hundred years."[71] It is an art form traditionally associated with women and is viewed as a way women maintain contact with one another and create a community amongst themselves. Semiotically, Roach explains a quilt has four functions: "as a practical household object, as an object or means of social interaction and family reaffirmation and continuation, as an art object, and as a vehicle to express cultural beliefs and worldview."[72] Each of these functions, in some way, assisted the AIDS Quilt in achieving its power. The codes that are linked to quilting are similarly linked to the AIDS Quilt. In comparison to other memorials, unity is at the very core of a quilt. It is literally the bringing together of pieces in order to create a whole. Similarly, the goal of the Quilt was to bring people together to become unified in the fight against AIDS. Hence, like a baseball game, quilting was a very effective and familiar code to call upon in order to create a powerful symbol. The planners activate connotations associated with quilts and quilting by using this particular symbolic form as an AIDS memorial. As a result, the negative connotations of AIDS were challenged by the positive connotations of a quilt (e.g., warmth, security, love, unity).

"Stop the Church" also involved a familiar code. However, unlike a baseball game or a quilt, the church is not considered popular or folk culture. It is a sacred, controlling institution in our society. Additionally, it is an extremely powerful symbol and has a strong impact not only on the lives of Catholics, but also on politics. Members of the church hierarchy (e.g., the Pope, Bishops, and Cardinals) are considered by many to be second only to God. And because church officials are one obvious means through which people can reach God, their opinions are often respected and rarely challenged. Also, because freedom to worship is one of the founding principles of our country, a challenge to this basic right results in responses that usually override any other issues that are raised. Each of these statements helps explain the codes through which the demonstration was read.

What the activists attempted to do was impose a new code on an already heavily-coded reality. During the demonstration, the activists attempted to portray Cardinal O'Connor and the church as evil by accusing them of being racist and homophobic. As an example, one particular graphic used during the demonstration reflects the demonic image of O'Connor the activists were attempting to present. In the picture O'Connor's eyes are covered by spirals reminiscent of the tools that villains often use when attempting to hypnotize others.

If the people witnessing the demonstration did not share the political views of the activists (and for those who were in the church such an agreement is highly unlikely), they viewed these new codes or representations of O'Connor and the Church as unfair. If, on the other hand, they shared the political orientation of the activists, this demonic representation was most likely viewed as something positive and rather humorous as well, as was the case for all of the activists whether or not they agreed with the decision to enter the church.

Thus, "Condom Day" and the Quilt introduced new codes in order to understand AIDS, and the codes within which these new codes were operating already had positive connotations for their respective audiences. In the "Stop the Church" demonstration, the activists attempted to do the same thing; however, because the Catholic Church as an institution is so heavily coded, the new AIDS code the activists wanted to convey was unable to overpower the preexisting codes associated with the Catholic Church.

Did the performances promote social change? Did they succeed in challenging the misrepresentations of AIDS that exist in the dominant culture? I will begin with the ACT UP demonstrations and conclude with the Quilt.

In his article on AIDS activism, Josh Gamson discusses the theatrical nature of ACT UP's demonstrations and how these performances attempt to change how AIDS is viewed by society. He states:

> ACT UP operates largely by staging events and by carefully constructing and publicizing symbols; it attacks the dominant representations of AIDS and of people with AIDS and makes attempts to replace them with alternative representations. At times, ACT UP attacks the representations alone; at times the attack is combined with a direct one on cultural producers and the process of AIDS-image production.[73]

Thus, as Gamson argues, ACT UP attempts to re-signify the constructions of AIDS presented by the dominant culture by attacking both the producers and the images related to AIDS. However, while ACT UP's performances are attempting to intervene in the signifying chain, their overall effectiveness is largely determined by how the mass media (re)presents their performances to society.

Of course, some ACT UP members recuperate "success" at a different level. In addition to those comments cited earlier, another member of ACT UP says at the end of the *Stop the Church* documentary:

> I thought the "Stop the Church" action was enormously successful . . . because what it did was get the issues into the public conversation, and that was our aim—not to change people's minds in the hierarchy of the church, not to make people think something in particular, but to start the conversation, to get these issues talked about. And that's what we did enormously successfully.

This woman's comments defines "success" in terms of raising issues rather than changing attitudes.

Obviously, raising issues is a necessary first step in the process of correcting misrepresentations. However, this demonstration, while minimally accomplishing the former (freedom of protest versus freedom to worship was the primary issue that was raised), failed to challenge the dominant discourse surrounding AIDS. While the demonstrators were able to get the issues talked about, the manner in which they were discussed (as is evident in the mass media's presentation of the demonstration) perpetuated the dominant discourse on AIDS rather than challenging it. In fact, the demonstration was not very successful in raising issues, let alone resignifying AIDS, because of how the media treated the demonstration. Additionally, the demonstrators who entered the church, most of whom were male, probably helped solidify the link in the parishioners minds between AIDS and homosexuality. Such a conclusion is supported by one woman's response included in the video. She states, "If they would only behave themselves they wouldn't get into this mess."

As I mentioned earlier, O'Connor was ready for ACT UP. He had staged his own performance and foiled their plan. I would argue that O'Connor's own performance and the one he staged using those attending the mass as a cast (as well as the media coverage of the performance) prevented the demonstration from achieving success. Instead, O'Connor succeeded in stifling ACT UP's voice within the church. He took the power away from the activists. The success of the demonstration was additionally hampered by the tactics utilized by ACT UP members—most notably, the decision to protest in the church. Hence, in the media, the AIDS issue was overshadowed by the controversy over constitutional rights. The issue became which right is more important—the freedom to worship or the freedom to protest.

During the post-demonstration discussion of "Stop the Church," one member of ACT UP declared, "I think we fucked up seriously . . . and I'm not scared of it. But there were 4500 people out there who didn't get their message across, and that is a problem."[74] This individual articulates the problem that plagued the demonstration and hampered its effectiveness—their message did not get across. Based on the media's response (which is, of course, related to the means through which Cardinal O'Connor handled the affair), freedom to worship superseded the freedom to protest. The AIDS message did not get across. The dominant perception of AIDS was maintained.

For "Condom Day," on the other hand, the media did not significantly intervene. The lack of coverage limited the audience for the protest to those attending the game. In addition, the activists challenged the belief that AIDS is a "gay disease" by targeting heterosexual men for their message—not men who were part of the dominant culture, but men who are often marginalized due to their socioeconomic status. The radical, but non-confrontational, tactics used by the demonstrators were effective in getting this message across. They used every means available—chants, billboards, and fliers—but did not interrupt the game. Thus, it could be argued that, although the audience was relatively small, the demonstration, especially in comparison to "Stop the Church," was successful because of the way it inserted these new codes of AIDS into the codes of the baseball game and into the audience's understanding of the virus.

However, I think this conclusion is complicated when a comparison is drawn between the "Stop the Church" demonstration and the production of *The Normal Heart* that occurred in Springfield. "Stop the Church" did force a number of issues into the public forum. That is, the AIDS issue did enter into the public discourse of the crisis. From this perspective, "Stop the Church" may be viewed as a more effective vehicle in the fight against AIDS than "Condom Day" because the latter, which had a smaller audience, never entered the public arena. Like the Springfield incident, the "Stop the Church" demonstration prompted much debate, and the recent controversy over Hilferty's video suggests that the issue remains. But unlike the Springfield incident, these debates occurred in more than one community.

Of the three performances, displays of the AIDS Quilt, I believe, are perhaps the most successful in terms of promoting social change. Because the Quilt does not discriminate among those who are represented, it serves to challenge the signifying chain established by the dominant discourse that equates AIDS with homosexuality and the belief that AIDS is solely a sexually transmitted disease. Also, because it is a quilt, it signifies traditional values, and creates a link between what quilting signifies and what the AIDS Quilt represents. And the amount of people who have experienced the Quilt gives it the potential to have the greatest effect on the AIDS crisis. It is a visual image that captures attention and creates a powerful response in those who see it. And the media's response to the Quilt has been largely positive. For the most part, the media attention has not reduced AIDS to an affliction of IV drug users or homosexuals; instead, it represents our society as a whole and the losses we have experienced as a result of the AIDS epidemic.

The Quilt, therefore, is an excellent example of a text that has not necessarily controlled the mass media, but it certainly has not been controlled by it. And if a group can get the mass media to present its message, without changing it to suit the dominant culture, it has accomplished a major goal in attempting to liberate society from the meanings and values of the dominant culture, which, in turn, can liberate those oppressed and marginalized members of society.

COMPARISONS AND CONCLUSIONS

As performances, these demonstrations had the potential to affect all those involved. For ACT UP members, these events allowed them to challenge dominant constructions and beliefs about AIDS, and express their anger at various institutions that have been (and still are) slow to respond to the crisis. As a result, they feel satisfied with their performances. As one activist stated after the St. Patrick's demonstration, "my favorite part was afterwards. . . . It was just one of those nice moments that happens when you do things in activism, where there isn't any reason for what you're doing, it's just an expression of collective joy or power."[75] For the activists, every performance, regardless of the outcome, makes them feel as though they have accomplished something in the fight against AIDS. If nothing else, these performances allow them to express their anger and outrage at a time when people they know and care about are dying because of a lack of attention.

Those who create panels for the NAMES Project receive a different type of satisfaction. Although the role they play is different from ACT UP members, their participation makes them feel, like the activists, as though they doing something in the fight against AIDS. However, while the activists are more concerned with the living in order to prevent more people from dying, those who create the panels are concerned with memorializing those who have died. It is their hope that their work will inspire others to make a panel or find other ways to help fight AIDS. Regardless of their motives, all those involved in these AIDS-related performances feel that they are accomplishing some goal.[76]

For the audiences, all these performances had the potential to infiltrate at the most basic level—language—and therefore, according to cultural studies theorists, had the power to produce social change. While each of these performances attempted to re-signify AIDS, "Condom Day" and the Quilt were clearly more effective. The "Stop the Church" demonstration, while attempting to challenge O'Connor and the church's representations on a number of issues, was not as carefully planned and executed. Or, it could be argued, this demonstration was planned and executed with different goals or strategies. It was met with a performance more deeply ingrained in the minds (and language) of the audience and thus, in the end, cannot be viewed as successful. While it did bring attention to the AIDS issue, one has to question what good "Stop the Church" did. Yes, it got people to talk about the issue, but it did not succeed in changing the dominant representations of AIDS. I can find no evidence to suggest that this demonstration infiltrated the dominant discourse surrounding AIDS.

The demonstration at Shea Stadium had a broader, unsuspecting target, and the activists apparently thought through every detail of the demonstration. The activists showed these baseball fans that AIDS is not just "a gay disease," that safe sex is not solely the woman's responsibility, and that safe sex needs to be as important to people as America's favorite pastime. Obviously, the number of people reached by this demonstration, especially given its lack of coverage on a national level, was not as large as the church demonstration. However, these small, successful demonstrations, such as the demonstration at Shea Stadium, are a step toward achieving the ultimate goal of ACT UP—ending the AIDS epidemic.

Finally, those who view the AIDS Quilt are also affected by the display. In fact, those who view the performance are not traditional audience members or performers; however, they do perform. For example, Jensen, quoting Cleve Jones, explains that peoples' behaviors change as they near the Quilt:

> Laughing men arriving from a tea dance sober quickly; uptight, suspicious teenagers soften and open. Everyone is silent by the time they reach the first canvas walkway. The people who say they're going to walk around it once are the people who stay six hours.[77]

The stigma surrounding AIDS is replaced by experiencing the Quilt. Grief, it is hoped, will turn into some kind of action in the fight against AIDS. Even a person who, for some reason, finds it extremely difficult to deal with the stigma attached to AIDS can be persuaded to take action. Jensen provides one of the best examples of the impact of the Quilt:

> In Kansas City, a man threatened over the telephone to come with a gun and "start shooting" unless a panel made by a friend of his dead son was taken down. Despite further threats of arson and lawsuits, the man and his wife were finally persuaded to visit the quilt. After walking slowly among the 2000 panels in Municipal Auditorium, they apologized, made a financial contribution, and said they were going home to make their own panel for their son.[78]

The response of this man to the Quilt suggests that it is a powerful and moving symbol—that his experience with the Quilt led him to take action in the fight against AIDS.

By comparison, it is unlikely that an individual who has such strong feelings about AIDS would be moved to take such direct action after witnessing an ACT UP demonstration, especially one like "Stop the Church." However, some ACT UP members feel that their type of action is much more productive than the Quilt. An ACT UP pamphlet contains the following statement: "We are through making quilts. We have already made our quilts, and each one says, 'I made this quilt while I was alive, so that you people could spend time demonstrating and lobbying rather than sewing.'"[79]

In conclusion, the issue of militancy versus mourning is quite relevant to the three performances discussed in this chapter. ACT UP members, as a whole, feel that the Quilt is not as strong a weapon as direct action in the fight against AIDS. However, as the responses to the Quilt reveal, while making a Quilt or viewing the Quilt is not the type of direct action engaged in by ACT UP, it can lead people to revise their thoughts about AIDS and result in direct action in the fight against AIDS.

NOTES

1. Bronski 223.

2. These two demonstrations selected for discussion are not meant to be representative of all of ACT UP's work. The sheer number of projects ACT UP has undertaken since its beginning would make it impossible to discuss each of them. However, I have chosen these two demonstrations because they differ from each other in regards to their immediate goals, their audience, and their reception (especially by the mass media).

3. Information regarding the history of the Names Project was taken from *The Quilt: Stories From the NAMES Project*, by Cindy Ruskin. The book provides both the history of the project, and tells the stories of some of the people who created the panels as well as those who are memorialized by them.

4. Moscone was a state senator and in 1975 was elected mayor. His "progay voting record" made him very popular among the gays and lesbians in San Francisco (D'Emilio, "Gay Politics" 468). Milk, who was openly gay, was elected city supervisor in a largely gay district of San Francisco in November of 1976. Both were murdered in 1978 by Dan White, a former city supervisor.

5. D. Walsh D13.

6. Ruskin 9.

7. These three goals, cited in Rozema and Brashers, are taken from information printed in the *NAMESletter*, a publication sponsored by the NAMES Project.

8. Ctd. in Rozema and Brashers 3.

9. Kramer, *Reports* 135.

10. Crimp and Rolston 28.

11. Crimp and Rolston 37.

12. Crimp and Rolston 53.

13. Crimp and Rolston 13.

14. Crimp and Rolston 15.

15. Baker 57.

16. In December of 1987, I witnessed, for the first time, a display of the Quilt in New York City's Central Park. The lack of

attention the Quilt received in subsequent displays, combined with my experience during this display and others since then, are two reasons why I chose to include the Quilt in this chapter. I should note, however, that the last display of all the panels of the Quilt in Washington in October 1992 did receive quite a bit of coverage in the mainstream press. But it would be difficult to ignore something which, at that time, included 20,064 panels, covered 15 acres, and weighed 26 tons (Yang 7A).

17. Ford F5. All information on pre-tour arrangements was obtained from Ford. While he is referring specifically to the 1988 tour, the information he presents is applicable to all of the displays that occur during the tours.

18. *Heart Strings* does not always occur simultaneously with the display of the Quilt. Sometimes, in fact, Act One occurs after Act Two.

19. DIFFA, founded in 1984, provides grants for AIDS/HIV organizations. DIFFA also assists corporations who want to provide support for AIDS/HIV-related projects and organizations. The foundation provided money for The Names Project, and also gave the Project the fabric and ties that surround individual blocks.

20. NAMES Project 4.

21. This information was obtained from various newspaper reports describing the display; see Jackler, Schneider, Stepanek, Yang.

22. Roland 38-43.

23. Unless otherwise noted, information about this demonstration was taken from Crimp and Rolston's *AIDS Demographics* (53-65).

24. Crimp and Rolston 62.

25. Crimp and Rolston 65.

26. Information for this section was taken from the following sources: Crimp and Rolston, DeParle, Gamson, Handleman, Magnuson, Kramer (Interview), and *Stop the Church*.

27. *Stop the Church*, a documentary on the demonstration by Robert Hilferty, provides one of the best descriptions of the event, including how decisions about the demonstration were made and what occurred after. In fact, it seems that one of the purposes of the

documentary was not only to show why the church needed to be stopped, but also to justify the actions of those who went into the church (actions that were later brutally misrepresented, according to some, by the press). The subsequent controversy produced by the video itself is discussed shortly.

28. Crimp and Rolston 140.

29. *Stop the Church*.

30. Bauer 257.

31. The cartoon and part of the article can be found in Crimp (259).

32. Ctd. in Crimp 257-59.

33. Baker 124. Baker's apparent surprise at the Quilt being referred to as rhetoric is somewhat surprising.

34. E. Zimmerman 19.

35. Clark 18.

36. Clark 21-22.

37. "Patchwork Memorial" 49.

38. "Patchwork Memorial" 49.

39. "Best of America" 59.

40. Gentry 550.

41. Gentry 551.

42. Gentry 550.

43. Fuchs 408.

44. Fuchs 409. Bronski makes a similar point about the Quilt when he argues that it "seems not only a concrete memorial but a way for all of us to acknowledge and deal with our pain, as well as a call to action" (228).

45. I am not arguing that Fuchs ignores the emotional nature of the Quilt. However, unlike others who have written about it, Fuchs links this "alternative expression of grief," as she calls it, to political action. The politics of the Quilt, she argues, has to do with the naming of those who have died. She states, "The quilt visibly resists the forces that make invisible the lives of those at risk from AIDS" (408).

46. Fuchs 409.

47. Biemiller A30.

48. At the end of the article, Fuchs quotes someone from the NAMES Project who said, "This is more than a quilt—it's a movement" ("The AIDS Quilt" 409). Although she does not make any comparisons between the work of other groups involved in ending the AIDS crisis, she does imply that this "movement" parallels demonstrations by various groups throughout the country.

49. Fuchs, "Performance" 17.

50. Baker 135.

51. One of the most melodramatic articles appears in the *Washington Times*. It begins, "They called out the first of the names of the AIDS dead Saturday morning on the Ellipse while the moon was still a sliver in the early-morning sky" (Donohoe F1).

52. Ford F4.

53. Donohoe F1.

54. Bronski 225.

55. However, one person interviewed explains that she became extremely angry after viewing the Quilt. She states, "It makes me angry, especially in this setting where you feel there are people who can do something about it" (Raines E11).

56. Gamson 351. Even the *New York Times* gave no mention of the demonstration in either the local news or the sports section on May 5 or 6, 1988. While the game between the Astros and the Mets was discussed, there was no mention of anything "out of the ordinary" in any of the articles.

57. This article, written by Eloise Salholz, is discussed in the final section of this chapter.

58. Morgan B4.

59. The different descriptions of the wafer incident in the mass media are rather interesting. The "desecration of the host" was the primary focus of most of the media coverage. However, what exactly happened to wafer is unclear. One says he destroyed it (Kramer, "Interview"), another said he dropped it (Crimp and Rolston), another said he threw it (Magnuson), still another said he crumbled it (DeParle). An Associated Press article quoted the church's rector as saying, "They threw or spat consecrated communion wafers to the floor of the cathedral," suggesting that *all* the activists were involved in this activity

("Judge Bars" 8D). For obvious reasons, the video on the demonstration, *Stop the Church*, does not touch upon this aspect.

60. Crimp and Rolston 138.

61. Crimp and Rolston 138.

62. Crimp and Rolston 138; DeParle B4.

63. Coleman 533.

64. Mahony A50.

65. *Stop the Church*. This philosophy is evident in ACT UP's disruption of the *CBS Evening News* during the Gulf War. At the beginning of one broadcast, a few members of ACT UP who had found a way to get into the station got in front of the cameras and shouted "Fight AIDS, not Arabs."

66. Sullivan 25.

67. In fact, when ACT UP and WHAM! wanted to go into the church on the anniversary of the demonstration, a New York City judge issued a restraining order against them ("Judge Bars" 8D). Because they wanted to celebrate the anniversary of this demonstration, it is clear that at least some of the members viewed it as a success.

68. All events designated performance art do not occur in spaces designated as theaters. Many occur in spaces such as galleries or parks. However, Finley's and Miller's performances did occur in rather traditional spaces. Hence, the comparisons mentioned are based solely on the space in which they were performed and not the texts themselves. As I suggested in chapter 3, the performance texts of Finley and Miller are the primary means through which they differentiate themselves from the plays discussed in chapter 2.

69. I do not mean to imply that the graphics utilized during "Stop the Church" were not effective. The point I am trying to make is that, overall, the choices made for the "Condom Day" demonstration seemed to be made more carefully. While the graphics for "Stop the Church" were effective, they seemed to be overshadowed by everything else that occurred.

70. Qtd. in Salholz 42.

71. Roach 54.

72. Roach 64.

73. Gamson 355.

74. Handleman 116.

75. Handleman 117.

76. I realize that I have spent little time discussing those who make the panels and those who participate in ACT UP's demonstrations. I include the previous information to show that regardless of how successful the display is, those who are the creators are deeply affected by their participation. The majority of these people, especially the AIDS activists, are those who attempt to change the dominant opinions about AIDS. They already understand, through personal experience, the impact that these misconceptions have on individuals and groups in society.

77. Ctd. in Rozema and Brashers 5.

78. Ctd. in Rozema and Brashers 5.

79. Ctd. in Rozema and Brashers 5.

V

Conclusion

[A]rt *does* have the power to save lives, and it is this very power
that must be recognized, fostered, and supported in every way
possible. But if we are to do this, we will have to abandon the
idealist conception of art. We don't need a cultural renaissance; we
need cultural practices actively participating in the struggle against
AIDS.[1]

As Douglas Crimp's quote suggests, art can participate in the
struggle for social change. Each of the performances discussed in this
study are examples of the cultural practices to which Crimp refers. And
in this study I have explored how these specific performances function
politically.

In this final chapter, I draw some conclusions regarding the
efficacy of performance for social change from a cultural studies
perspective. Additionally, I discuss the limitations inherent in this
perspective derived from this study as they relate to an understanding
of any performance event.

The primary conclusion to be drawn from this study is that
there is no definitive, essential way to talk about performance and social
change. It is only when we look at specific performances, how they are
received, circulated, debated, or ignored, that we can begin to
understand whether or to what extent they reproduce or challenge
existing systems of power and authority. As this study indicates, there
are numerous factors to consider when attempting to understand the
rhetoric of performance. Each element of the performance interacts with
the others in comprising the performance event. In other words, a
performance cannot be studied without looking at the context in which
it occurs, the form the performance takes, and the content of the
performance itself. And, when all these factors are taken into

consideration, it becomes clear that there is no direct correlation—no cause/effect relationship—between performance and social change.

It is impossible to argue, as Larry Kramer wishes to do, that his play is a significant artifact in the history of AIDS. Because there are so many communities where his play did not spark the controversy that occurred in Springfield, one cannot argue that any of these performances, in and of themselves, is significant in the fight against AIDS. In a more general sense, while some may argue that performances can promote revolutionary changes, the findings of this study suggest that performances are, as Boal states, rehearsals for revolution[2]—that "having rehearsed a resistance to oppression will prepare [participants] to resist effectively in a future reality, when the occasion presents itself once more."[3]

Similarly, the analyses of these performances reveal some limitations in regards to the cultural studies perspective. While theorists working from this perspective argue that "re-signifying" or "deconstructing" the dominant discourse of AIDS will change the way people behave, the findings of this study suggest that changing behavior is not as simple as these theorists argue. That is, as I suggested above, there are many more issues that must be considered. The results of the Springfield incident and the "Stop the Church" demonstration imply that when these issues are publicly debated, when sites outside the immediate performance context are created for discussion, it becomes possible for social change to occur.

The elements of the performance attended to by those reading it largely determine the conclusions that can be drawn. Thus, the political effectiveness of these performances depends upon how they are interpreted, especially by the mass media. And, as the responses to all of these performances suggest, the mass media plays a gatekeeping role; that is, in most cases, the media makes these performances safe for the "general population." As a result, the media limits both the resignifying power and political potential of these performances.

In *Theatrewritings*, Bonnie Marranca discusses the important role that critics play with regards to the success of any performance.[4] She argues that critics "shape the audience's attitude toward the arts . . . " regardless of whether or not the critics understand what the work is about.[5] As a result, critics determine how audiences read the performance event and, at a more basic level, they often determine whether or not people will choose to see a performance. For each of the performances discussed in this study, regardless of their form, the critical responses, for the most part, attempted to present them in a way that made them acceptable for the mainstream.

This "making-the-performance-safe" is most obvious in the reviews that stress the universality of the issues the performance raises. In the responses to *As Is* and *The Normal Heart*, this approach was most apparent—everyone can understand love and death; thus, most people can find these performances pleasurable and cathartic experiences. For Karen Finley, the reviews made sure the audiences understood the nature of performance art, explaining its relationship to theatre and, in doing so, allowed the audience to read the performance through a lens they already understand—that of traditional theatre—even though there exist definite distinctions between the two. Additionally, the mass of publicity she received led to audiences composed of some who did not allow her to make her point. For Tim Miller, the lack of attention afforded his performance protects the audience from the work. For if they did not know about his work, they would not be inclined to see it; however, this lack of publicity allowed his audience to remain partial and more prone to having their consciousness raised.

The responses to the ACT UP demonstrations also reflect the idea that the media serve a gatekeeping role. The reporters either ignored the demonstration (as in the case of "Condom Day") or they condemned the entire demonstration because the issues raised challenge the authority of a sacred institution (as in "Stop the Church"). The responses to the Quilt also provided this safety net by either ignoring it (because the reporters do not know what to do with it) or invoking the universality theme that is apparent in the responses to the plays—everyone can understand what it means to lose someone. Additionally, the Quilt is represented as a way to mourn the loss of those who have died from AIDS and purge the mourners of their feelings, which may include guilt, without forcing them to engage in any direct action.

Still, while both critics and reporters arguably played a gatekeeping role in preparing the audience for the performances, they did not prevent people from actually witnessing these performances, especially in the case of ACT UP. Instead, the responses to these events often served as interpretations for those who did not see them. And these interpretations reinforce dominant perceptions about AIDS either through a conscious lack of attention or by viewing the demonstration from the perspective of the person whom they considered to be the more credible source—Cardinal O'Connor.

Additionally, the audience's reading formation affects their responses to these events. Audience members who do not reject these performances may diminish or dilute them by shaping them into the kind of theatrical event, such as a play in the mode of classic realism, that allows for pleasure and emotional release. Within this space even the avant-garde performances of Finley and Miller may be unable to challenge the reading formation that is so deeply ingrained in the audience. For those who were familiar with performance art prior to the NEA controversy, the response is probably different; for these audience members, however, it could be argued that the performances cannot produce the desired effect because most of the audience members are partial to the issues that are presented. Performances occurring in traditional theatre spaces, regardless of their form, often end up "preaching to the converted." However, as I have suggested, sometimes these performances serve a "consciousness-raising function" that may assist in the process of social change.

Other difficulties affecting the efficacy of performance involve the ephemeral nature of the performance event. While performance is generally considered a less commodifiable art form, its ephemeral nature makes it difficult to talk about. Not only is it difficult to define what a performance is, it is often difficult to "freeze" it, except through the mediation of other technical devices that inevitably change the event and what it means. For example, neither a videotape nor a written text is an accurate representation of the entire performance. A video distinguishes the performance from its "present-tenseness" and further changes the event by focusing in on some elements of the performance and ignoring others. Focusing on the written text also poses similar problems in that it ignores the impact that the performance context has on its audience and also ignores the fact that no two performances are ever the same, even if they are working from a pre-written text.

The conclusions to be drawn from this study suggest that each performance occurs in a specific time and place. Essentially, the way any performance is read is largely determined by the codes that are in place as part of the performance event. Social change involves understanding and then challenging the theatrical and societal codes that have been imbedded in the event. As Janet Wolff explains, we must understand "*how* codes represent reality to us . . . in order to provide alternatives which expose rather than reflect reality.[6]" This study reveals how these codes represent our reality and suggests some alternatives that Wolff's assertion demands.

Performances, while they can be effective, are not likely to promote revolutionary changes in society. While they may assist in this process, one specific performance can never be viewed as causing a revolution. Each performance is a cultural event. However, whether the performance will maintain or challenge the status quo depends upon many factors.

I now return to the issue of AIDS. Judith Williamson argues:

> It is only as familiar structures of meaning are shaken and taken apart that new ones can form. And looking at things differently makes it possible to *act* differently. The hackneyed scenarios through which we make sense of many things are challenged by the advent of AIDS. As we find ways to confront the syndrome itself that challenge and the changes it can bring are surely worth rising to.[7]

Each of these performances is an attempt to shake these structures and to teach us to act differently. However, such a perspective on social change is problematic because it suggests that new meanings are inherently linked to changes in behavior. As this study indicates, social change is a complex issue. But each attempt at artistic intervention has the potential to assist us in the "long revolution" of social change, on which, in the drama of the AIDS crisis, the curtain has yet to fall.

NOTES

1. Crimp, "AIDS" 7.

2. Boal 141.

3. Boal 150.

4. Although she refers specifically to *Einstein on the Beach*, an avant-garde performance in the late 1970s, Marranca makes a number of helpful points that relate to the role theatre critics play regardless of the performance they are reviewing.

5. Marranca 116.

6. Wolff 90.

7. Williamson 80.

Bibliography

Acker, Kathy. "On Top of a Peak." *Newstatesman and Society* 11 May
    1990: 42-43.

Adorno, Theodor W. "Culture Industry Reconsidered." Alexander and
    Seidman 275-82.

Alexander, Jeffrey C. "Analytical Debates: Understanding the Relative
    Autonomy of Culture." *Culture and Society: Contemporary
    Debates*. Ed. Jeffrey Alexander and Steven Seidman.
    Cambridge: Cambridge UP, 1990. 1-27.

Altman, Dennis. *AIDS in the Mind of America: The Social, Political,
    and Psychological Impact of a New Epidemic*. New York:
    Anchor, 1986.

Andrews, Robert M. "NEA Awards $47 Million in Grants to 1,200
    Artists, Arts Organizations." *Morning Advocate* [Baton Rouge,
    LA] 5 Jan 1991: 6B.

Averback, Howard. "Media's Effect: From Play to Event." Paper
    presented at the Speech Communication Association
    convention. Chicago, 2 Nov. 1990.

Baker, Rob. *The Art of AIDS*. New York: Continuum, 1994.

Barish, Jonas. *The Anti-theatrical Prejudice*. Berkeley: U of California
    P, 1981.

Barnes, Clive. "Healthy Production of *As Is*." Rev. of *As Is*, by William
    M. Hoffman. *New York Times* 12 Mar. 1985: 50.

——. "Joel Grey Adds Love to the AIDS Equation." *New York Post* 8 Oct. 1985: 61.

——. "Plague, Play, and Tract." Rev. of *The Normal Heart*, by Larry Kramer. *New York Post* 5 May 1985: 12.

Belsey, Catherine. *Critical Practice*. London: Methuen, 1980.

Benjamin, Walter. "The Work of Art in the Age of Mechanical Reproduction." *Illuminations*. Ed. Hannah Arendt. Trans. Harry Zohn. New York: Schocken, 1968. 217-51.

Bennett, Susan. *Theatre Audiences: A Theory of Production and Reception*. New York: Routledge, 1990.

"Best of America: The Culture." *U.S. News and World Report* 9 July 1990: 59-60.

Bibby, Bruce. "Hello, Larry: Superstars Opine on Kramer." *POZ* April/May 1995: 42+.

Biemiller, Lawrence. "For 3 Days at Dartmouth, Panels of the AIDS Memorial Quilt Bring Tears, Memories, and a Riot of Color to 8,700 Visitors." *Chronicle of Higher Education* 29 May 1991: A28-30.

Boal, Augusto. *Theatre of the Oppressed*. Trans. Charles A. and Maria-Odilia Leal McBride. New York: Theatre Communications Group, 1985.

Bowman, Michael, and Della Pollock. "'This Spectacular Visible Body': Politics and Postmodernism in Pina Bausch's *Tanztheater*. *Text and Performance Quarterly* 9 (1989): 113-118.

Bradley, Robert H. "The Abnormal Affair of *The Normal Heart*." Paper presented at the Speech Communication Association convention. Chicago, 2 Nov. 1990.

Brandes, Phillip. "Apple Pie Roots." *Los Angeles Times* 7 February, 1991.

Brantlinger, Patrick. *Crusoe's Footprints: Cultural Studies in Britain and America*. New York: Routledge, 1990.

Brecht, Bertolt. *Brecht on Theatre: The Development of an Aesthetic*. Trans. John Willett. New York: Hill and Wang, 1964.

Breslauer, Jan. "Art=Activism." *Los Angeles Times* 1 Dec. 1991. NewsBank SOC 108: A1-A7.

Brockett, Oscar G. *History of the Theatre*. 5th ed. Boston: Allyn and Bacon, 1987.

Bronski, Michael. "Death and the Erotic Imagination." Carter and Watney 219-28.

Bumbalo, Victor. "A Play About People: William M. Hoffman Talks About His New Play, *As Is*." *New York Native* 24 Mar. 1985: 31-33.

Burnham, Linda Frye. "Angels on Your Shoulders: A Conversation with Tim Miller about Art and Activism." *Art Papers* Jan./Feb. 1990: 10-15.

Burns, Elizabeth. *Theatricality: A Study of Convention in the Theatre and Social Life*. New York: Harper, 1972.

Callahan, Tom. "Stunned by Magic: A True American Hero Joins the Battle Against the Deadly AIDS Virus." *U.S. News and World Report* 18 Nov. 1991: 82-84.

Capecci, John. "Performing the Second Person." *Text and Performance Quarterly* 1 (1989): 42-52.

Carter, Erica, and Simon Watney, eds. *Taking Liberties: AIDS and Cultural Politics*. London: Serpent's Tail, 1989.

Case, Sue-Ellen, ed. *Performing Feminisms: Feminist Theory and Theatre*. Baltimore: Johns Hopkins, 1990.

Clark, Gilbert. "Art in the Schizophrenic Fast Lane: A Response." *Art Education* 43.6 (1990): 8-23.

Clements, Marcelle. "Karen Finley's Rage, Pain, Hate and Hope." *New York Times* 22 July 1990, sec. 2: 1+.

Clum, John M. "'A Culture That Isn't Just Sexual': Dramatizing Gay Male History." *Theatre Journal* 41 (1989): 169-89.

Coffey, Michael. "Karen Finley's Disembodied Texts from City Lights." Rev. of *Shock Treatment*, by Karen Finley. *Publishers Weekly* 14 Sept. 1990: 90.

Coleman, John A. "ACT-UP v. The Church: Sex, Lies and That Videotape." *Commonweal* 27 Sept. 1991: 533-35.

Collins, Jim. *Uncommon Cultures: Popular Culture and Post-Modernism*. New York: Routledge, 1989.

Combs, James E., and Michael W. Mansfield, eds. *Drama in Life: The Uses of Communication in Society*. New York: Hastings, 1976.

Conquergood, Dwight. "Poetics, Play, Process, and Power: The Performative Turn in Anthropology." *Text and Performance Quarterly* 1 (1989): 82-95.

Crimp, Douglas, ed. *AIDS: Cultural Analysis/Cultural Activism.* Cambridge, MA: MIT P, 1988.

——. "AIDS: Cultural Analysis/Cultural Activism." Crimp, *Cultural Analysis* 3-16.

——. "How to Have Promiscuity in an Epidemic." Crimp, *Cultural Analysis* 237-71.

——. "Mourning and Militancy." *October* 51 (1989): 3-18.

Crimp, Douglas, and Adam Rolston. *AIDS Demographics.* Seattle: Bay Press, 1990.

D'Emilio, John. *Sexual Politics, Sexual Communities: The Making of a Homosexual Minority in the United States, 1940-1970.* Chicago: U of Chicago P, 1983.

——. "Gay Politics and Community in San Francisco Since World War II." *Hidden From History: Reclaiming the Gay and Lesbian Past.* Ed. Martin Bauml Duberman, Martha Vicinis, and George Chauncey, Jr. New York: New American Library, 1989. 456-73.

DeParle, Jason. "Rude, Rash, Effective, Act-Up Shifts AIDS Policy." *New York Times* 3 Jan. 1990: B1+.

De Vries, Hilary. "All the Rage." *Los Angeles Times* 21 Oct. 1990. NewsBank PEO 56: F6.

Dolan, Jill. *The Feminist Spectator as Critic.* Ann Arbor: UMI Research P, 1988.

Donohoe, Cathryn. "AIDS Quilt Stirs Marchers." *Washington Times* 10 Oct. 1988. NewsBank HEA 128: F1-2.

Eagleton, Terry. *Marxism and Literary Criticism*. Berkeley: U of California P, 1976.

Ehrenfeld, Tom. "AIDS 'Heroes' and 'Villains.'" *Newsweek* 14 Oct. 1991: 10.

Elson, John. "The Dangerous World of Wannabes." *Time* 25 Nov. 1991: 77+.

Evans, Rowland, and Robert Novak. "The NEA's Suicide Charge." *Washington Post* 11 May 1990: A27.

Faust, Gretchen. "New York in Review." Rev. of *We Keep Our Victims Ready*, by Karen Finley. *Arts Magazine* Oct. 1990: 120.

Feingold, Michael. "Anger Unbound." Rev. of *We Keep Our Victims Ready*, by Karen Finley. *Village Voice* 9 Oct. 1990: 105+.

———. Introduction. *The Way We Live Now: American Plays and the AIDS Crisis*. Ed. M. Elizabeth Osborn. New York: Theatre Communications Group, 1990. xi-xvii.

Fettner, Ann Giudici. "Heart Minus Snarl." Rev. of *The Normal Heart*, by Larry Kramer. *New York Native*. 21-27 Oct. 1985: 40.

Fine, Elizabeth C., and Jean Haskell Speer. "A New Look at Performance." *Communication Monographs* 44 (1977): 374-89.

Finley, Karen. *The Constant State of Desire. Shock Treatment*. San Francisco: City Lights, 1990. 1-26.

———. Interview. By Kirk W. Fuoss. Unpublished, 1992: 1-9.

———. "Karen Finley: A Constant State of Becoming." Interview. By Richard Schechner. *Drama Review* 32.1 (1988): 152-58.

———. Letter. *Drama Review* 34.2 (1990): 9-10.

———. "Our Beating Hearts." *Artforum* Sept. 1990: 21.

———. *We Keep Our Victims Ready. Shock Treatment.* San Francisco: City Lights, 1990. 103-44.

Fiske, John. *Understanding Popular Culture.* Boston: Unwin Hyman, 1989.

Ford, David. "AIDS Quilt: Stitches in Time." *San Francisco Examiner* 3 Apr. 1988. NewsBank HEA 45: F4-6.

Forte, Jeanie. "Women's Performance Art: Feminism and Postmodernism." Case 251-69.

Fuchs, Elinor. "The AIDS Quilt." *Nation* 31 Oct. 1988: 408-9.

———. "The Performance of Mourning." *American Theatre.* January 1993: 15-18.

Gaggi, Silvio. *Modern/Postmodern: A Study in Twentieth-Century Arts and Ideas.* Philadelphia: U of Pennsylvania P, 1989.

Gallagher, John. "The AIDS Media Circus: Hype and Hysteria Behind the Headlines." *Advocate* 10 Sept. 1991: 32-37.

Gamson, Josh. "Silence, Death, and the Invisible Enemy: AIDS Activism and Social Movement 'Newness.'" *Social Problems* 36 (1989): 351-66.

Gentry, Jerry. "The NAMES Project: A Catharsis of Grief." *Christian Century* 24 May 1989: 550-51.

Gevisser, Mark. "Gay Theater Today." *Theatre* 21 (Summer/Fall 1990): 46-51.

Gilman, Sander L. "AIDS and Syphilis: The Iconography of Disease." Crimp, *Cultural Analysis* 87-108.

Glueck, Grace. "Border Skirmish: Art and Politics." *New York Times* 19 Nov. 1989: H1+.

Goldberg, Rosa Lee. *Performance Art: From Futurism to the Present.* Rev. ed. New York: Abrams, 1988.

Goldstein, Richard. "The Implicated and the Immune: Responses to AIDS in the Arts and Popular Culture." *A Disease of Society: Cultural and Institutional Responses to AIDS.* Ed. Dorothy Nelkin, David P. Willis, and Scott V. Parris. Cambridge: Cambridge UP, 1991. 17-42.

———. "Kramer's Complaint." *Village Voice* 2 July 1985: 20+.

Green, Judith. "Karen Finley: Art on the Edge." *San Jose Mercury News* 17 Feb. 1991. NewsBank PEO 8: D14.

Greif, Martin. *The Gay Book of Days.* Secaucus, NJ: Lyle Stuart, 1982.

Grossberg, Lawrence. "Strategies of Marxist Cultural Interpretation." *Critical Studies in Mass Communication* 1 (1984): 392-421.

Grover, Jan Zita. "AIDS: Keywords." Crimp, *Cultural Analysis* 17-30.

Gussow, Mel. "Sensitive Material Presented With Compassion." Rev. of *As Is,* by William M. Hoffman. *New York Times* 31 Mar. 1985, sec. 2: 3.

Haden-Guest, Anthony. "Live Art: Annie Leibovitz Photographs Five Women Who Shock." *Vanity Fair* Apr. 1992: 205-12.

Hall, Richard. "The Transparent Closet: Gay Theater for Straight Audiences." *Three Plays for a Gay Theater and Three Essays.* San Francisco: Grey Fox, 1983. 171-77.

Hall, Stuart. "Cultural Studies: Two Paradigms." *Media, Culture, and Society.* Ed. Richard Collins, et al. Beverly Hills: Sage, 1986. 33-48.

Handleman, David. "ACT UP in Anger." *Rolling Stone* 8 Mar. 1990: 80+.

Hanson, Henry. "Karen Finley: Performance Provocateur." *Chicago* Oct. 1990: 23-24.

Havelock, Eric A. *Preface to Plato.* Cambridge: Harvard UP, 1963.

Henry, William A. III. "A Common Bond of Suffering." Rev. of *As Is,* by William M. Hoffman, and *The Normal Heart,* by Larry Kramer. *Time* 13 May 1985: 85.

Hermassi, Karen. *Polity and Theater in Historical Perspective.* Berkeley: U of California P, 1977.

Heuvel, Michael Vanden. *Performing Drama/Dramatizing Performance: Alternative Theater and the Dramatic Text.* Ann Arbor: U of Michigan P, 1991.

Hoffman, William M. *As Is. The Way We Live Now: American Plays and the AIDS Crisis.* Ed. M. Elizabeth Osborn. New York: Theatre Communications Group, 1990. 3-62.

Holleran, Andrew. Introduction. *The Normal Heart.* Kramer 23-28.

HopKins, Mary Frances, and Leon Perkins. "Second-Person Point of View." *Critical Survey of Short Fiction.* Ed. Frank Magill. Englewood Cliffs: Salem, 1981. 119-32.

Hughes, Robert. "Whose Art is it Anyway?" *Time* 4 June 1990: 46-48.

Huyssen, Andreas. *After the Great Divide: Modernism, Mass Culture, Postmodernism.* Bloomington: Indiana UP, 1986.

Jackler, Rosalind. "Rain, Tears Flow at Washington Site of AIDS Quilt as Unfurling Delayed." *Houston Post* 10 Oct. 1992: A19.

Jacobs, Laura. "Of Angels and Witches." *New Leader* 29 Oct. 1990: 22-23.

Jameson, Fredric. "Reflections on the Brecht-Lukács Debate." *The Ideologies of Theory: Essays 1971-1986, Volume 2: The Syntax of History.* Vol. 49 of *Theory and History of Literature.* Minneapolis: U of Minnesota P, 1988. 133-47.

Johnson, Magic. Interview. *Prime Time Live.* By Connie Chung. 11 Dec. 1991.

———. Interview. *The Arsenio Hall Show.* ABC. 8 Nov. 1991.

Joseph, Miranda. Letter. *Drama Review* 34.4 (1990): 13-16.

Jowitt, Deborah. "Get on Board." Rev. of *Stretch Marks,* by Tim Miller. *Village Voice* 29 May 1990: 113-14.

"Judge Bars AIDS, Abortion Protesters from Disrupting Services at Cathedral." *Sunday Advocate* [Baton Rouge, LA] 9 Dec. 1990: 8D.

Kalb, Jonathan. "We Keep Our PR Ready." Rev. of *We Keep Our Victims Ready,* by Karen Finley, and *Rameau's Nephew,* by Denis Diderot. *Village Voice* 2 Oct. 1990: 112.

Keating, Douglas J. "Tim Miller Performs at the Painted Bird." Rev. of *Sex/Love/Stories*, by Tim Miller. *Philadelphia Inquirer* 8 June 1991. N. pag.

Kepke, Allen N., and Ronald E. Shields. "From Chronicle to Social History: Interpreting Public Ceremony as Theatre History." *Text and Performance Quarterly* 10 (1990): 324-30.

Kleinberg, Seymour. "Life After Death." *The New Republic* 11-18 August 1986: 28-33.

Koehler, Robert. "*Normal Heart* Stirs Up the Heartland." *Los Angeles Times* 3 December 1989, 41+.

Kramer, Larry. Interview. "Using Rage to Fight the Plague." By Janice C. Simpson. *Time* 5 Feb. 1990: 7-8.

——. Introduction. *Just Say No: A Play About a Farce*. New York: St. Martin's, 1989. ix-xxiv.

——. *The Normal Heart*. New York: Plume, 1985.

——. *Reports From the Holocaust: The Making of an AIDS Activist*. New York: St. Martin's, 1989.

Kroll, Jack. "Going to the Heart of AIDS." Rev. of *As Is*, by William M. Hoffman, and *The Normal Heart*, by Larry Kramer. *Newsweek* 13 May 1985: 87+.

Larson, Kay. "Censor Deprivation." *New York Magazine* 6 Aug. 1990: 48-49.

Levine, Ira A. *Left-Wing Dramatic Theory in the American Theatre*. Ann Arbor: UMI Research P, 1985.

Linn, Amy. "Karen Finley." *Philadelphia Inquirer* 7 Apr. 1991. NewsBank PEO 12: C2-D1.

Longtime Companion. Prod. Stan Wlodkowski. Dir. Norman René. Companion Productions and American Playhouse Theatrical Films, 1990. 96 min.

Lynes, Russell. *The Lively Audience: A Social History of the Visual and Performing Arts in America, 1890-1950.* New York: Harper, 1985.

MacCabe, Colin. "Realism and the Cinema: Notes on Some Brechtian Theses." *Screen* 15.2 (1974): 7-27.

Magnuson, Ed. "In a Rage Over AIDS: A Militant Group Targets the Catholic Church." *Time* 25 Dec. 1989: 33.

Mahony, Roger. "A Case of Bigotry?: An Open Letter to the People of Southern California." Advertisement. *Los Angeles Times* 6 September 1991: A50.

Manischewitz, Leora. "Theatre: *As Is* Author Seeking Resolution, Self-Healing." *Villager* 30 May 1985: 15.

Marcuse, Herbert. *The Aesthetic Dimension.* Boston: Beacon, 1978.

Marranca, Bonnie. *Theatrewritings.* New York: Performing Arts Journal, 1984.

"Martina: Magic's Message Wrong." *Arizona Republic* [Phoenix, AZ] 21 Nov. 1991: A1.

Massa, Robert. "T-Cells and Sympathy." Rev. of *As Is,* by William Hoffman. *Village Voice,* 25 Mar. 1986: 89.

Merla, Patrick. "Triumph Over Death: Circle Repertory Company's Revival of *As Is* Is an Occasion For Joy." Rev. of *As Is*, by William M. Hoffman. *New York Native* 1 June 1987: 29+.

Mesce, Deborah. "NEA Chief Says Sexually Explicit Art to Have Trouble Getting Funding." *The Advocate* [Baton Rouge, LA] 6 May 1992: 2A.

Messinger, Sheldon L., Harold Simpson, and Robert D. Towne. "Life as Theatre: Some Notes on the Dramaturgic Approach to Social Reality." Combs and Mansfield, 73-83.

Miller, Tim. *Stretch Marks. Drama Review* 35.3 (1991): 143-70.

Moore, Frank. Letter. *Drama Review* 35.1 (1991): 14-17.

Morgan, Thomas. "Mainstream Strategy for AIDS Group." *New York Times* 22 July 1988: B1+.

Mukerji, Chandra, and Michael Schudson. *Rethinking Popular Culture: Contemporary Perspectives in Cultural Studies*. Berkeley: U of California P, 1991.

Mulvey, Laura. "Visual Pleasure and Narrative Cinema." *Screen* 16.3 (1975): 6-18.

Mygatt, T. Rev. of *Stretch Marks*, by Tim Miller. *Backstage* 25 May 1990: 28A.

Mygatt, Thomas. "Performance Artists Fly Into Storm Amid Lawsuits and Controversy." *Backstage* 5 Oct. 1990: 38.

Nadotti, Maria. "Karen Finley's Poisoned Meatloaf." *Artforum* Mar. 1988: 113-116.

"NAMES Project AIDS Memorial Quilt: Loving Memories that Educate and Inspire." Houston: AIDS Foundation of Houston, 1995.

NAMES Project Foundation. "An Event in 3 Acts: The National Tour," 1992.

Natalle, Elizabeth J. *Feminist Theatre: A Study in Persuasion.* Metuchen, NJ: Scarecrow, 1985.

Overn, Michael. Letter to the author. 29 Oct. 1991.

"The Patchwork Memorial." *Time* 10 Oct. 1988: 49.

Patton, Cindy. *Inventing AIDS.* New York: Routledge, 1990.

Phelan, Peggy. "Money Talks, Again." *Drama Review* 35.3 (1991): 131-41.

Pollock, Della. Introduction. *The Aesthetics and Anti-Aesthetics of Postmodern Performance: Pina Bausch's Tanztheater. Text and Performance Quarterly* 9 (1989): 97-98.

Poovey, Mary. "Cultural Criticism: Past and Present." *College English* 52 (1990): 615-25.

Radetsky, Peter. "The First Case." *Discover* 12.1 (1991): 74-75.

Raines, George. "Quilt a Balm to the Living." *San Francisco Examiner* 10 Oct. 1988. NewsBank HEA 128: E11.

Roach, Susan. "The Kinship Quilt: An Ethnographic Semiotic Analysis of a Quilting Bee." *Women's Folklore, Women's Culture.* Ed. Rosan A. Jordan and Susan J. Kalcik. Philadelphia: U of Pennsylvania P, 1985. 54-64.

Roland, Eric L. "Keeping the Love Alive: The NAMES Project Quilt." *Out Smart* 15 Mar.-14 Apr. 1995: 38-43.

Rozema, Hazel J. and Dale Brashers. "Quilts vs. Chains: A Comparison of Symbolic Strategies in the AIDS Movement." Paper presented at the Popular Culture Association convention. San Antonio, 29 Mar. 1991.

Ruskin, Cindy. *The Quilt: Stories From the NAMES Project.* New York: Pocket Books, 1988.

Salholz, Eloise. "Acting UP to Fight AIDS: A Group's Angry Tactics." *Newsweek* 6 June 1988: 42.

Salisbury, Stephan. "A Gay, Political All-American Boy." *Philadelphia Inquirer* 7 June 1991: 1D+.

Sante, Luc. "Blood and Chocolate." *New Republic* 15 Oct. 1990: 34-37.

Sayre, Henry S. *The Object of Performance: The American Avant-Garde Since 1970.* Chicago: U of Chicago P, 1989.

Scarupa, Henry. "Reading of Names from AIDS Quilt Will Mark End of its Cross-Country Tour." *Sun* [Baltimore, MD] 7 October 1988. NewsBank HEA 128: E14.

Schechner, Richard. *Between Theatre and Anthropology.* Philadelphia: U of Philadelphia P, 1985.

——. *The End of Humanism: Writings on Performance.* New York: Performing Arts Journal Publications, 1982.

——. *Performance Theory.* Rev. ed. New York: Routledge, 1988.

——. "Political Realities, the Enemy Within, the NEA, and You." *Drama Review* 34.4 (1990): 7-10.

Schneider, Howard. "Candlelight March, Speeches Cap Day of Viewing AIDS Quilt." *Houston Chronicle* 11 Oct. 1992: 10A.

Schuler, Catherine. "Spectator Response and Comprehension: The Problem of Karen Finley's *Constant State of Desire.*" *Drama Review* 34.1 (1990): 131-45.

Shapiro, Laura. "A One-Woman Tour of Hell." Rev. of *We Keep Our Victims Ready*, by Karen Finley. *Newsweek* 6 Aug. 1990: 60-61.

Shapiro, Michael J. *The Politics of Representation: Writing Practices in Biography, Photography, and Policy Analysis.* Madison: U of Wisconsin P, 1988.

Shewey, Don. Introduction. *Out Front: Contemporary Gay and Lesbian Plays.* Ed. Shewey. New York: Grove, 1988. xi-xxvii.

Shilts, Randy. *And the Band Played On.* New York: St. Martin's, 1987.

Span, Paula, and Carla Hall. "At Home with the NEA 4." *American Theatre* 7.6 (1990): 14-21.

Spillane, Margaret. "The Culture of Narcissism." *Nation* 10 Dec. 1990: 737-40.

Stallybrass, Peter, and Allon White. *The Politics and Poetics of Transgression.* Ithaca: U of Cornell P, 1986.

Stam, Robert. *Reflexivity in Film and Literature: From Don Quixote to Jean-Luc Godard.* Ann Arbor: UMI Research P, 1985.

Stepanek, Marcia. "AIDS Quilt: A Work of Love, Protest." *Houston Chronicle* 9 Oct. 1992: 12A.

Stop the Church. Videocassette. Dir. and prod. Robert Hilferty. Altar Ego Productions, 1990.

Sullivan, Andrew. "Gay Life, Gay Death." *New Republic* 17 Dec. 1990: 19-25.

Swift, E. M. "Dangerous Games." *Sports Illustrated* 18 Nov. 1991: 41-43.

Syna, Sy. "*The Normal Heart* Offensive and Boring." Rev. of *The Normal Heart*, by Larry Kramer. *New York City Tribune* 22 April 1985: 6B.

Tongues Untied. Dir. and prod. Marlon Riggs. PBS, 1989.

Treichler, Paula A. "AIDS, Gender, and Biomedical Discourse: Current Contests for Meaning." *AIDS: The Burdens of History.* Ed. Elizabeth Fee and Daniel M. Fox. Berkeley: U of California P, 1988. 190-266.

———. "AIDS, Homophobia, and Biomedical Discourse: An Epidemic of Signification." Crimp, *Cultural Analysis* 31-70.

———. "How to Have Theory in An Epidemic: The Evolution of AIDS Treatment Activism." *Technoculture.* Ed. Constance Penley and Andrew Ross. Minneapolis: U of Minneapolis Press, 1991. 57-106.

Turner, Graeme. *British Cultural Studies: An Introduction.* Boston: Unwin Hyman, 1990.

Turner, Victor. *The Anthropology of Performance.* New York: Performance Art Journal Publications, 1987.

van Erven, Eugène. *Radical People's Theatre.* Bloomington: Indiana UP, 1988.

Wallis, Brian. Introduction. *Art After Modernism: Rethinking Representation.* Ed. Wallis. New York: New Museum of Contemporary Art. Boston: Godine, 1984. xi-xviii.

Walsh, Diana. "AIDS Quilt Coming Home 4 Times Bigger." *San Francisco Examiner* 20 Nov. 1988. NewsBank HEA 155: D13.

Walsh, Thomas. "NEA Grants for Finley and Hughes Okd By Council." *Backstage* 16 Sept. 1990: 3+.

Watney, Simon. "AIDS, Language and the Third World." Carter and Watney 183-92.

——. *Policing Desire: Pornography, AIDS, and the Media.* Minneapolis: U of Minneapolis Press, 1987.

——. "Taking Liberties: An Introduction." Carter and Watney 11-57.

Watts, Harriett. "The Dada Event: From Transubstantiation to Bones and Barking." *"Event" Arts and Art Events.* Ed. Stephen C. Foster. Ann Arbor: UMI Research P, 1988. 119-31.

Weales, Gerald. "AIDS on Stage: Advocacy and Ovations." Rev. of *As Is*, by William M. Hoffman, and *The Normal Heart*, by Larry Kramer. *Commonwealth* 10 July 1985: 406.

Williams, Raymond. *The Long Revolution.* London: Chatto and Windus, 1961.

——. *Marxism and Literature.* Oxford: Oxford UP, 1977.

Williamson, Judith. "Every Virus Tells a Story: The Meaning of HIV and AIDS." Carter and Watney 69-80.

Wilmoth, Charles. "Karen Finley: *We Keep Our Victims Ready.*" *High Performance* 49.1 (1990): 57.

Wolff, Janet. *The Social Production of Art.* New York: New York UP, 1981.

Wright, Elizabeth. *Postmodern Brecht: A Re-Presentation.* New York: Routledge, 1989.

Yang, John E. "20,000 Silent Messages Woven into AIDS Quilt for D.C. Display." *Houston Chronicle* 20 Sept. 1992.

Zimmerman, David. "Arts 'Decency' Standards Ruled Invalid." *USA Today* 10 June 1992: 1A.

Zimmerman, Enid. "Questions About Multiculture and Art Education or 'I'll Never Forget the Day M'Blawi Stumbled on the Work of the Post-Impressionists." *Art Education* 43.6 (1990): 8-24.

Index